An Introduction to

Fair Use and Copyright Management of Universities in India

An introduction to
Fair Use and Copyright Management of Universities in India

Sabuj Kumar Chaudhuri
University of Calcutta
India

Ess Ess Publications
New Delhi

An introduction to
Fair Use and Copyright Management of Universities in India

ISBN: 978-81-933597-4-7

First Published 2017

Published by:
Ess Ess Publications
4831/24, Ansari Road,
Darya Ganj,
New Delhi-110 002.
INDIA
Phones: 23260807, 41563444
Fax: 41563334
E-mail: info@essessreference.com
www.essessreference.com

Cover Design by *Patch Creative Unit*

Printed and bound in India at Salasar Imaging Systems.

AFFECTIONATELY DEDICATED
To
MY WIFE and SON
Barnali and Saraswata

Contents

Annexure

Foreword

It's a pleasure to write a short foreword for this book, which I think will be very helpful for faculty members, researcher and students of any discipline, staff and the whole creative community of any university. University survives academically on new creation and innovation that finally diffuse in the society to fuel progression of human civilization. We are living in a different world of internet at least wherefrom we started our journey in the world without internet. In this Google era content creation, distribution and its consumption has become very common to any average person. But the basic values attached to creative work remain same. Some people fear or avoid copyright laws as an impediment of teaching-learning process. But philosophical premise behind copyright says just contrary to it. Copyright, one of the most important forms of Intellectual Property Rights (IPR) is granted to protect exclusive rights of creators and at the same time it conceived fair use provisions for users of copyrighted works so that it can facilitate and initiate future creations. Free riding to any copyrighted work is not permitted by copyright laws of any country. In fact, safety valve is already provided in Indian Copyright Act as fair dealing provisions in Section 52. We need to explore this section or any such flexibility exist in our law in a better way than ever before to put ourselves on the right path and to avoid undesirable law suit. So far I understand, scare, confusion, anxiety prevails in our university community regarding copyright act. But, it is poorly highlighted fair dealing route as savior and is able to provide enough flexibilities and alternatives to the university community that may promote fearless teaching-learning and scholarship. This book has focused that unaddressed and poorly studied area i.e., fair use of copyrighted works and also designed a model copyright management policy for a university. This book will not only be welcomed by the university community across India and its neighboring countries but equally it will be of immense help for academic administrators to device a policy to promote and exercise fair use in universities in the years to come. I believe this book will unbolt a new beginning of copyright-compliant creative community in our universities for what we are aspiring for a long time.

Prof. Swagata Sen
Pro-Vice-Chancellor (for Academic Affairs)
University of Calcutta, India

Preface

I have had immense pleasure writing this book which is not because of a sense of accomplishment but a sense of serving to the academic mission of higher education in India. Journey to reach this feat was not smooth at all. Ups and downs of life and familial mishaps sometimes deflected me but could never stop me from speaking my mind. This book is my contribution to the academic community aimed at making them aware of fair use of the copyrighted works. Universities are considered as the breeding ground of new knowledge and it must be created in fair way keeping law on the right side. I know there are miles to go before we can make our students, researchers and even faculty members of universities fully aware to respect the creation and the rights of creators so that the same can be reciprocated in due course. I will be happy if this book at least can initiate the journey among the academic community.

In Chapter One *Introduction to Copyright and Fair Use*, the subject of Intellectual Property Rights (IPR) has been introduced to readers. Copyright is one of the most important acts by which creative works are protected by the government. Besides, other forms of IPR have also been briefly discussed. Genesis of Indian Copyright Act including various provisions and definitions has been lucidly narrated avoiding legal jargon as much as possible. Chapter ends with the provisions of fair use in our laws.

Chapter two *Concept of Fair Use* commences with the history of copyright to enable the readers to understand its rationale and importance in creativity. Being the core chapter of this book, the concept of fair use has been fully explored and unfolded with its philosophical basis and check-list as a savior to keep users of copyrighted works within the legal limits. For those who might be confused, *four factor analysis* for fair use has been detailed with clarifications and required format as ready reference. Several classic international and national cases have been examined to understand the complexities of the issues involved.

In Chapter three *Copyright and Universities,* the indispensible interconnectivity between university and copyright has been explained. Core mission of any educational institution is the exchange of ideas and development of new knowledge. This is why we find these everyday expressions in various forms of intellectual outputs which demand legal protection over them. At the same time, academic community is the biggest consumer of the creative works produced outside of the university system. Balancing the interest of stakeholders is very crucial in the creative process and to achieve the goal of a university.

Chapter four *(Un)Fair use in the Universities?* unfurls a disturbing story before readers which was the finding of two years study sponsored by the University Grants Commission of the Government of India through its minor research project grant. This study was conducted among 20 universities in West Bengal among teachers, students, research scholars and librarians. It revealed that we are lacking true copyright culture in our universities which is detrimental not only for qualitative research output but it may also invite unwanted legal hassles in the future. This kind of copyright defying teaching-learning system in our universities is what is responsible for our falling stature in the higher educational map of the world.

Chapter five *Designing a Copyright Management Policy for Universities* stretches out one of the most important aspirations of this book. Lack of true creative culture in our universities may be one of the reasons that attest the absence of any visible well-defined copyright management policy in our universities. Copyright compliant universities in the USA, UK and in Europe show us the benefit of innovation and creation. A model policy for copyright management has been designed, inspired from universities of the countries that lead the way in copyright law enforcement.

Chapter six *Fair Use in SAARC Countries* compares the fair use or fair dealing provisions in SAARC countries. This comparison will help readers to understand how copyrighted works are used legitimately in our neighboring countries having more or less same socio-economic and cultural background.

Chapter seven *Fair Use Guidelines,* the last chapter of this book unravels the guidelines for all stakeholders in the university community to keep them within the justifiable boundary and inspire them for maximum utilization of flexibility as given in our copyright law for the promotion of scholarship and advancement of learning.

— Sabuj Kumar Chaudhuri

Acknowledgements

Any work of serious endeavour requires inputs of all types and this has come to me as and when required. I acknowledge the help, attention, cooperation, support, patience and even criticism that so many people have generously offered me over the years that have made this project possible. Words fail me in expressing enough gratitude to all such people.

I always received internal motivation from my late father and mother.

I received continuous appreciation and utmost encouragement from my son Saraswata and my wife Barnali while I toiled on this book. without their constant support, this book would not have seen the light of the day. I am deeply indebted to the editorial team led by Sumit Sethi of Ess Ess Publications who took the pain to publish this work. Last but not the least, I seek forgiveness of all those who have been with me over the course of the years and whose names I have failed to mention.

— Sabuj kumar Chaudhuri

Glossary

Adaptation : Adaptation involves the preparation of a new work in the same or different form based upon an already existing work.

Assign : In assigning the economic rights, the creator gives the rights of the work in perpetuity to the new copyright owner with or without remuneration.

Author : Creator of literary, dramatic, artistic, sound recordings, cinematographic, photographic or computer programs.

Copyright : Copyright is a right given by the law to creators of literary, dramatic, musical and artistic works and producers of cinematograph films and sound recordings. In fact, it is a bundle of rights including, *inter alia,* rights of reproduction, communication to the public, adaptation and translation of the work. There could be slight variations in the composition of the rights depending on the work.

Creative Commons : Copyright licenses and tools offer a balance inside the traditional "all rights reserved" to "some rights reserved" setting that copyright law creates.

Derivative work : A derivative work is a work based on or derived from one or more already existing works.

E-resources : Resources that can be accessed with a computer. May be stored on CD-ROM

Gross Domestic Product (GDP) : The total market value of all final goods and services produced in a country in a given year, equal to total consumers, investment and government spending, plus the value of exports, minus the value of imports. GDP is commonly used as an indicator of the economic health of a country, as well as to gauge a country's standard of living.

Fair Dealing : Subject to certain conditions, a fair deal for research, study, criticism, review and news reporting, as well as use of works in library and schools and in the legislatures, is permitted without specific permission of the copyright owners. In order to protect the interests of users, some exemptions have been prescribed in respect of specific uses of works enjoying copyright.

Fair Use : Analogous term of fair dealing in the US Copyright Act.

Infringement : Copyright infringement involves any violation of the exclusive rights of the copyright owner.

Intangible property : It includes a list of products of human intellect such as patents, copyright, trademarks and industrial designs, etc.

Intellectual Property : Intellectual property is a cluster of legally recognized rights associated with innovation and creativity – the works of the mind, as against physical products, land and other tangible resources.

Intellectual Property Rights : Rights awarded by society to individuals or organizations over inventions, literary and artistic works, and symbols, names, images, and designs used in commerce. They give the titleholder the right to prevent others from making unauthorized use of their property for a limited period.

Joint Authorship : Work of joint authorship means a work produced by the collaboration of two or more authors in which the contribution of one author is not distinct from the contribution of the other author or authors.

License : A license is a long-term agreement that allows use of the material under particular conditions and payments, but the copyright is retained by the creator.

Plagiarism : The reproduction or appropriation of someone else's work without proper attribution; passing off as one's own the work of someone else is plagiarism.

Property : The term is extraordinarily difficult to answer. Ordinary person defines property as 'thing' but attorney defines it as 'right'. It has two understandings legal understandings and economic understandings.

Reserve : In reserving the rights, the creator withholds certain rights from assigning or licensing

Purchasing Power Parity (PPP) : An economic theory that estimates the amount of adjustment needed on the exchange rate between countries in order for the exchange to be equivalent to each currency's purchasing power. In other words, the exchange rate adjusts so that an identical good in two different countries has the same price when expressed in the same currency.

Reproduction : The right of reproduction commonly means that no person shall make one or more copies of a work or of a substantial part of it in any material form including sound and film recording without the permission of the copyright owner. The most common kind of reproduction is printing an edition of a work. Reproduction occurs in storing of a work in the computer memory.

Scholarship : Scholarship is the craft of learning and teaching (activities that encompass research and creative expression).

Stakeholders : Stakeholders can affect or be affected by the organization's actions, objectives and policies.

Tangible property : It includes physical objects such as land, household goods, car, etc.

Tempe Principles : The 'Tempe Principles' related with copyright management in the universities that were adopted in Tempe, Arizona, on March 2-4, 2000, at a conference sponsored by the Association of American Universities, the Association of Research Libraries, and the Merrill Advanced Studies Center of the University of Kansas.

Transformation : Re-purposing of the original copyrighted work develops a transformative work through the mechanism of transformation.

Zwolle Principles : The Group developed seven 'Principles' aimed at 'balancing stakeholder interests in scholarship-friendly copyright practices'. To assist stakeholders—including authors, publishers, librarians, universities and the public—to achieve maximum access to scholarship without compromising quality or academic freedom and without denying aspects of costs and rewards involved.

1

Introduction to Copyright and Fair Use

Fair use is always going to be a gray area, and it should be. We need to allow for things we can't see yet.

— Robin Gross

(*Famous American Lawyer*)

1.0. Introduction

Before plunging into the subject of fair use, interesting and a bit complex as well, I would like to make clear first few basic concepts regarding intellectual property rights and copyrights. The interplay between fair dealing or fair use and copyright is an extremely complex issue that calls for a cohesive and logical understanding of the subject. In the next few paragraphs, we will try to learn the basics of copyright and interpretation and explanation of few conceptual terms. Then we gradually enter to the realm of fair use. Let us explore...

What is Intellectual Property Rights?

Intellectual property (IP) deals with the creations of the human intellect and protects the creations of the human mind, the human *intellect*. This is why this kind of property is called "intellectual" property". Intellectual property is a cluster of legally recognized rights associated with innovation and creativity – the works of the mind, as against physical products, land and other tangible resources. Even though it is intangible, intellectual property (IP) is often recognized as personal property, to be sold and traded like other forms of property.

But national laws normally don't define 'intellectual property' as a single property right. Instead, 'intellectual property' is used as a convenient general term describing a range of distinct legal rights. Within this spectrum, intellectual property rights (IPR) can be very different from one another, in their subject matter, in the way they are defined, administered and enforced, and in the way they impact on other people.

IP is categorized as Industrial Property (functional commercial innovations), and Artistic and Literary Property (Cultural creations). Copyright as one of the most important Intellectual property Rights (IPR) ensures certain minimum safeguards of the rights of authors over their creations, thereby protecting and rewarding creativity. Current technological developments are blurring, to some extent, this distinction, and some hybrid *sui generis* (Latin expression meaning "of its own kind") systems are emerging. Various forms of IPR have shown in the following *fig 1* [Commission on Intellectual Property Rights (CIPR), UK 2002]:

Fig. 1. Classification of IPR
(*Source* : CIPR)

Creativity being the keystone of progress, no civilized society can afford to ignore the basic requirement of encouraging the same. Economic and social development of a society is dependent on creativity. The protection provided by copyright to the efforts of writers, artists, designers, dramatists, musicians, architects and producers of sound recordings, cinematograph films and computer software, creates an atmosphere conducive to creativity, which induces them to create more and motivates others to create. To sum up, Intellectual property rights (IPR) are the rights awarded by society to individuals or organizations principally over Intellectual Property i.e., creative works: inventions, literary and artistic works, and symbols, names, images, and designs used in commerce. They give the creator the right to prevent others from making unauthorized use of their property for a limited period.

1.1. What is Copyright?

Copyright is one of the main branches of Intellectual Property Rights (IPR), grants authors and artists control over certain creations for defined periods of time. It limits who may copy, change, perform or share those creations. We can also say that copyright is a right given by the law to creators of literary, dramatic, musical and artistic works and producers of cinematograph films and sound recordings for a limited period of time. Copyright is a negative right that prevents one from copying.

Copyright protects "original works of authorship" that are fixed in a tangible form of expression or medium. The fixation need not be directly perceptible so long as it may be communicated with the aid of a machine or device. That medium can be almost anything, includ-ing paper, computer disk, clay, canvas, and so on. Copyright protection is not registered or applied for but instead protects the work from the moment that it has been created. Copyright does not protect the idea itself, but instead protects how the idea is expressed, arranged, formatted and even organized so long as the expression of the idea is represented with some form of physical permanency, and is original in scope.

The owner of copyright in a protected work may use the work as he wishes, and may prevent others from using it without his authorization. Thus, the rights granted under national laws to the owner of copyright in a protected work are normally "exclusive rights" to authorize others to use the work, subject to the legally recognized rights and interests of others.

1.2. Understanding Copyright

Idea behind Copyright

The idea behind copyright is rooted in certain fundamental ideas about creativity and possession. Basically, it springs from the idea that anything we create is an extension of 'self' and should be protected from general use by anyone else. Coupled with this is the idea that the person creating something has exclusive rights over the thing created, partly from economic reasons but also because of this extension of 'self' idea. Copyright is therefore important to ensure the continued growth of writing, performing and creating. If there were no copyright protection there would be little stimulus for people to create anything, as other people would be able to take the work and use it in any way they wanted. Copyright law aims to protect this growth but, at the same time, tries to ensure that some access to copyright works is allowed as well. Without this access creators will be starved of ideas and information to create more copyright materials (Cornish, 2009).

Genesis of Copyright in India

Modern copyright law developed in India gradually in three distinct phases spreading more than 150 years.

Phase I : 1847 Statute of the East India Company

Copyright law entered India in 1847 through an enactment during the East India Company's regime. According to the 1847 enactment, the term of copyright was for the lifetime of the author plus 7 years after his death. But in no case could the total term of copyright exceed a period of 42 years whichever happened to be longer. The government could grant a compulsory licence to publish a book if the owner of copyright, upon the death of the author, refused to allow its publication. Unlike today, copyright in a work was not automatic. Registration of copyright with the Home Office was mandatory for the enforcement of rights under the Act. However, the Act also specifically reserved the subsistence of copyright in the author, and his right to sue for its infringement. It was remained in force until it was repealed by the Copyright Act, 1911.

Phase II : 1914 Indian Copyright Act (UK Copyright Act, 1911 as template)

The Government of India considered that the early introduction of an Act into India was desirable not only for Imperial and international reasons but also for domestic reasons. In 1914, British India enacted a new Copyright Act which merely an extension of the United Kingdom Copyright Act of 1911 to India. There were 2 major changes in the act firstly, duration of copyright was modified and reduced to 10 years from the date of first publication and secondly, it introduced criminal sanctions for violation of copyright or copyright infringement. They also changed translation rights of authors' up to inexplicable extent for the promotion of publication industry in whole India that characterizes their distinct dominant colonial policy. But it had very detrimental impacts on authors as their plights observed by the experts. Say for example, two famous Bengali writers- works of Gurudev Rabindranath Tagore and Sarat Chandra Chattopadhya were translated in Hindi and other languages sold thousands of copies but authors did not receive a single penny for that.

Phase III : 1957 Indian Copyright Act (repealed Indian Copyright Act of 1914)

After the Act of 1914, there had been considerable and significant technological developments across the globe like gramophone records, cinematographs, sound and television and broadcasts etc.

With the passage of time, the necessity for a comprehensive act was keenly felt in India. In India, independence of India and constitutional changes were also influencing factors for enactment of new laws.

In India, the Copyright Act of 1957, was passed on 4th June, 1957 and came into force on 21st January, 1958. With the introduction of the Copyright Act of 1957, Indian Copyright Act of 1914 was completely repealed.

Criteria to get copyright

Works need to be tangible and original expression to become eligible for copyright. This means, for example, that a verbal presentation that is not recorded cannot be copyrighted. However, anything that is tangible can be copyrighted. There are three fundamental requirements for something to be copyrighted:

Fixation

The item must be fixed in some way. The fixation may be just about anything. For example, a piece of paper, a computer disk, an audiotape, or a videotape is all legitimate forms of fixation.

Originality

The work must be original. Originality includes a novel or a student's email message, facebook post to a professor's lecture notes. Both are considered examples of original expression. For a work to be "original," it must meet two qualifications: (1) it cannot be copied from another work; and (2) it must exhibit at least a small amount of creativity.

Minimal Creativity

The work must include something that is above and beyond the original.

Verbatim use is not considered original. Reference to the original work that is used to discuss a new concept would be considered original, however.

Creativity need only be extremely slight for the work to be eligible for protection.

To be protected, a work has to be more than a mere idea. The distinction between protected works and ideas lies at the very heart of copyright law. The protection of a given work applies to the expressions of ideas that are contained therein.

It is not necessary for the work to be completely original. Works may be combined, adapted, or transformed in new ways that would make them eligible for copyright protection.

Securing copyright

Acquisition of copyright is automatic and it does not require any formality. Copyright comes into existence as soon as a work is created and no formality is required to be completed for acquiring copyright. However, certificate of registration of copyright and the entries made therein serve as *prima facie* evidence in a court of law with reference to dispute relating to ownership of copyright

Any individual who is an author or rights owner or assignee or legal heir can file application for copyright of a work either at the copyright office or by post or by e-filing facility from the Copyright Office web-site *http://www.copyright.gov.in.*

Unpublished works and Copyright

Both published and unpublished works can be registered. Copyright in works published before 21st January, 1958, i.e., before the Copyright Act, 1957 came in force, can also be registered, provided the works still enjoy copyright. Three copies of published work may be sent along with the application. If the work to be registered is unpublished, a copy of the manuscript has to be sent along with the application for affixing the stamp of the Copyright Office in proof of the work having been registered. In case two copies of the manuscript are sent, one copy of the same duly stamped will be returned, while the other will be retained, as far as possible, in the Copyright Office for record and will be kept confidential. It would also be open to the applicant to send only extracts from the unpublished work instead of the whole manuscript and ask for the return of the extracts after being stamped with the seal of the Copyright Office.

When a work has been registered as unpublished and subsequently it is published, the applicant may apply for changes in particulars entered in the Register of Copyright in Form V with prescribed fee.

Whether computer software is copyrightable?

Computer Software or programme can be registered as a 'literary work'. As per Section 2 (o) of the Copyright Act, 1957 "literary work" includes computer programmes, tables and compilations, including computer databases. 'Source Code' has also to be supplied along with the application for registration of copyright for software products.

Terms of Copyright

Types of Work	Duration of Copyright
• Literary • dramatic, • musical and • artistic works	Lifetime of the author + 60 years from the beginning of the calendar year next following the year in which the author dies. Example: *if Author dies in say 2nd Nov, 2015. So, duration of protection of 60 years period will be counted from 1st Jan, 2016 to 31st Dec, 2076. Also, in case of joint author, year count for this process will depend upon the author who dies last. Example: Author X and Y are co-author of a work. Author X dies on 2nd April 2013 and Y dies on 16th August 2015. So duration of protection of sixty years period will start from 1st Jan, 2016.*
• Anonymous and pseudonymous works • Posthumous work • Cinematograph films • Sound records • Government work • Public undertakings • International Agencies • photographs	Until 60 years from the beginning of the calendar year next following the year in which the work is first published • period is counted from the date of first publication • Period starts from the beginning of next year, following the year in which film was first published.
• Performer's Right • Broadcaster's Right	25 Years

1.3. Copyright as Economic and Moral Right

There are two types of rights under copyright, economic rights, which allow the owner of rights to derive financial reward from the use of his works by others, and "moral rights," which allow the author to take certain actions to preserve the personal link between him and the work.

Copyright is an *economic* or *property right*; the creator can earn rewards from the efforts of their creative originality. In addition, it is a *moral* right that concerns the reputation or professional standing of the creator in the eyes of peers.

Economic Rights

Copyright is in essence a bundle of rights covering the following:

1. *Rights for reproduction,* i.e. exclusive rights to make copies of the work.
2. *Rights to publish,* i.e. this are the right to issue copies of the works to the public.
3. *Rights for rental and lending,* i.e. these are the rights to control the hiring or lending of a work or copy of the work to the public.
4. *Rights for modification/adaptation,* i.e. exclusive rights to modify and make adaptations and create derivative works.
5. *Right to translate,* i.e. exclusive right to translate so that any translator cannot reproduce or publish any translation without the appropriate consent from the owner of the copyright of the original work.
6. *Rights for distribution,* i.e. the rights distribute the work to the public.
7. Rights for public performance, i.e. the right to recite, play, dance, or act with or without the aid of a machine.
8. *Rights for public display,* i.e. the right to display the work anywhere that is open to the public
9. *Rights of communication to the public,* i.e. this is the new right to communicate literary, dramatic, musical, artistic, sound recordings, film or broadcast to the public by electronic communication.

Economic rights can be *licensed, assigned,* or *reserved.* In all situations, responsibilities and obligations of all parties should be outlined in a contract:

1. A *licence* is a long-term agreement that allows use of the material under particular conditions and payments, but the copyright is retained by the creator. For example, one university may allow another university to present a particular course in a particular environment on payment of a per student fee for five years. *A license simply means renting one's copyrighted work.*
2. In *assigning* the economic rights, the creator gives the rights of the work in perpetuity to the new copyright owner with or without remuneration. For example, one university or an academic writer could assign the rights of a particular course to another university with a one-time payment. *Assign simply means selling out one's copyrighted work.*
3. In *reserving* the rights, the creator withholds certain rights from assigning or licensing, for example, on-line delivery of materials. The originating university may license the print rights, but not allow the user to deliver that particular course electronically.

Moral Rights

Three important moral rights are normally identified in national legislation:

1. *The Right of Paternity* is the right to be identified as author or creator of the work. This right must be asserted in writing.
2. *The Right of Integrity* is the right not to have the work altered (as, for example, in the colour reproduction of a painting), presented in an unsuitable context, or otherwise treated in a 'derogatory' manner.
3. *The Right of False attribution* is the right not to have the work wrongly ascribed.
4. *The Right of Disclosure* is the right of the author to

withhold certain photographs or films from publication.

5. *The Right of Publication* is the right to decide whether or not to publish the work.

Moral rights remain with the creator and cannot be passed on to another copyright holder when assigning the economic rights. Moral rights are said to be 'inalienable'. Note that there are no moral rights for works carried out in the course of employment. Moral rights may become more of an issue with electronic forms of a work, which can be easily modified. Attribution is sometimes unclear with on-line materials.

1.4. Various Right for Various Classes of Work

In the case of a *literary work* (except computer programme), copyright means the exclusive right

- To reproduce the work
- To issue copies of the work to the public
- To perform the work in public
- To communicate the work to the public.
- To make cinematograph film or sound recording in respect of the work
- To make any translation of the original work
- To make any adaptation of the work.

Computer programmes are protected under the Copyright Act. They are treated as literary works.

In addition to all the rights applicable to a literary work, owner of the copyright in a computer programme enjoys the rights to sell or give on hire or offer for sale or hire, regardless of whether such a copy has been sold or given on hire on earlier occasion.

In the case of a *dramatic work*, copyright means the exclusive right

- To reproduce the work

- To communicate the work to the public or perform the work in public
- To issue copies of the work to the public
- To include the work in any cinematograph film
- To make any adaptation of the work
- To make translation of the work.

In the case of an *artistic work*, copyright means the exclusive right

- To reproduce the work
- To communicate the work to the public
- To issue copies of the work to the public
- To include the work in any cinematograph film
- To make any adaptation of the work.

In the case of a *musical work*, copyright means the exclusive right

- To reproduce the work
- To issue copies of the work to the public
- To perform the work in public
- To communicate the work to the public
- To make cinematograph film or sound recording in respect of the work
- To make any translation of the work
- To make any adaptation of the work.

In the case of a *cinematograph film*, copyright means the exclusive right

- To make a copy of the film including a photograph of any image forming part thereof
- To sell or give on hire or offer for sale or hire a copy of the film
- To communicate the cinematograph film to the public.

In the case of *sound recordings*, copyright means

the exclusive right

- To make any other sound recording embodying it
- To sell or give on hire, or offer for sale or hire, any copy of the sound recording
- To communicate the sound recording to the public.

1.5. Interpretations of Related Terms

Now interpretations of various related terms have been given in the following:

Author

(a) in relation to a literary or dramatic work, the author of the work

(b) in relation to a musical work, the composer

(c) in relation to an artistic work other than a photograph, the artist

(d) in relation to a photograph, the person taking the photograph

(e) in relation to cinematograph film or sound recording, the producer and

(f) in relation to any literary, dramatic, musical or artistic work which is computer generated, the person who causes the work to be created

Work

A work means any of the following, namely, a literary, dramatic, musical or artistic work, a cinematograph film, or a sound recording.

Work of Joint Authorship

"Work of joint authorship" means a work produced by the collaboration of two or more authors in which the contribution of one author is not distinct from the contribution of the other author or authors.

Government Work

"Government work" means a work which is made or published by or under the direction or control of

- the government or any department of the government
- any legislature in India, and
- any court, tribunal or other judicial authority in India.

Indian Work

"Indian work" means a literary, dramatic or musical work,

- the author of which is a citizen of India; or
- which is first published in India; or
- the author of which, in the case of an unpublished work is, at the time of the making of the work, a citizen of India.

Literary Work

Written down letter, word, list, course, novel, poem, translation, compilation, edition, computer program, tables, compilations and databases

Performance

Performance, in relation to performer's right, means any visual or acoustic presentation made live by one or more performers.

Performer

Performer includes an actor, singer, musician, dancer, acrobat, juggler, conjurer, snake charmer, a person delivering a lecture or any other person who makes a performance.

Artistic

Anything crafted by an artist in a two- or three-dimensional form whether or not any such work possesses artistic quality: painting, sculpture, photograph, illustration, chart, cartoon, typographical layout, drawing, technical drawing, map.

- a painting, a sculpture, a drawing (including a diagram, map, chart or plan), an engraving or a photograph, whether or not any such work possesses artistic quality;
- a work of architecture; and
- any other work of artistic craftsmanship.

Dramatic work

It includes any piece of recitation, choreographic work or entertainment in dumb show, the scenic arrangement or acting, form of which is fixed in writing or otherwise but does not include a cinematograph film.

Musical work

Work consisting of music and includes any graphical notation of such work but does not include any words or any action intended to be sung, spoken or performed with the music

Cinematograph Film

Any work of visual recording on any medium produced through a process from which a moving image may be produced by any means and includes a sound recording accompanying such visual recording and "cinematograph" shall be construed as including any work produced by any process analogous to cinematography including video films

Sound recording

It means a recording of sounds from which sounds may be produced regardless of the medium on which such recording is made or the method by which the sounds are produced. A phonogram and a CD-ROM are sound recordings.

Computer

It includes any electronic or similar device having information processing capabilities.

Computer programme

A set of instructions expressed in words, codes, schemes or in any other form, including a machine readable medium, capable of causing a computer to perform a particular task or achieve a particular result.

Broadcast

It means communication to the public by any means of wireless diffusion, whether in any one or more of the signs, sounds or visual images or by wire and includes rebroadcast.

Communication to the public

It simply means making any work available for being seen or heard or otherwise enjoyed by the public directly or by any means of display or diffusion other than by issuing copies of such work regardless of whether any member of the public actually sees, hears or otherwise enjoys the work so made available.

Lecture

It includes address, speech and sermon.

Delivery

In relation to a lecture, includes delivery by means of any mechanical instrument or by broadcast.

Reprography

It means the making copies of work, by photocopying or similar means.

Duplicating equipment

It means any mechanical contrivance or device used or intended to be used for making copies of any work.

Infringing Copy

In case of literary, dramatic, musical or artistic work, a reproduction will invite infringement

1 In case of cinematographic film, a copy of the film made on any medium by any means

2 In case of sound recording, any other recording embodying the same sound recording, made by any means

3 In relation to programme or performance reproduction, copy or sound recording is made or imported in contravention of the provisions of this Act.

Copyright Protection in Derivative Works

The copyright in a derivative work covers only the additions, changes, or other new material appearing for the first time in the work. Protection does not extend to any preexisting material, that is, previously published or previously registered works or works in the public domain or owned by a third party.

1.6. Some Deeper Understanding

Adaptation Vs Derivative Works

Indian Copyright Act, 1957 clarifies the term *'adaptation'* as

(i) Conversion of dramatic work into a non-dramatic work;

(ii) Conversion of the literary work or an artistic work into a dramatic work by way of performance in public or otherwise;

(iii) Any abridgement of the literary or dramatic work or any version of the work in which the story or action is conveyed wholly or mainly by means of pictures in a form suitable for reproduction in a book, or in a newspaper, magazine or similar periodical;

(iv) Any arrangement or transcription of the musical work; and

(v) Any use of such work involving its re-arrangement or alteration;

The US Copyright act has elaborately mentioned derivative work which is analogous to adaptation work by the Indian Copyright Act.

A derivative work is a work based on or derived from one or more already existing works. Common derivative works include translations, musical arrangements, motion picture versions of literary material or plays, art reproductions, abridgments, and condensations of pre-existing works. Another common type of derivative work is a "new edition" of a pre-existing work in which the editorial revisions, annotations, elaborations, or other modifications represent, as a whole, an original work. To be copyrightable, a derivative work must incorporate some or all of a pre-existing "work" and add new original copyrightable authorship to that work. The derivative work right is often referred to as the adaptation right. The following are examples of the many different types of derivative works:

- A motion picture based on a play or novel
- A translation of an novel written in English into another language
- A revision of a previously published book
- A sculpture based on a drawing
- A drawing based on a photograph
- A lithograph based on a painting
- A drama about John Doe based on the letters and journal entries of John Doe
- A musical arrangement of a pre-existing musical work
- A new version of an existing computer program
- An adaptation of a dramatic work
- A revision of a website

Transformativeness

Transformativeness is a characteristic of some derivative works that makes them transcend, or place in a new light, the underlying works on which they are based. In computer and Internet-related works, the transformative characteristic of the later work is that it provides the public with a benefit not previously available to it, which would otherwise remain unavailable. Such transformativeness weighs heavily in a fair use analysis and may excuse what seems a clear copyright infringement from liability. Transformative use of a copyrighted material does the following:

- Adds value to the copyrighted material
- Employs it for a purpose different from that for which it was originally intended or repurposed
- Can involve modifying material or putting material into a new context or recontextualized

Translation

Translation has not been defined in our Indian copyright act. It ordinarily means translation of text from one language to another. The copyright owner of the work is entitled to the translation right. There is nothing preventing a man from translating a work. The translator has copyright in translation. But he cannot reproduce or publish the translation without the consent of the owner of the copyright of original work.

Copyright Protection in Compilations and Collective Works

The copyright in a compilation of data extends only to the selection, coordination or arrangement of the materials or data, but not to the data itself. In the case of a collective work containing "preexisting works" works that were previously published, previously registered, or in the public domain—the registration will only extend to the selection, coordination or arrangement of those works, not to the preexisting works themselves.

Compilations

Compilations of data or compilations of preexisting works (also known as "collective works") may also be copyrightable if the materials are selected, coordinated, or arranged in such a way that the resulting work as a whole constitutes a new work. When the collecting of the preexisting material that makes up the compilation is a purely mechanical task with no element of original selection, coordination, or arrangement, such as a white-pages telephone directory, copyright protection for the compilation is not available. Some examples of compilations that may be copyrightable are:

- A directory of the best services in a geographic region
- A list of the best short stories of 2011
- A collection of sound recordings of the top hits of 2004
- A book of greatest news photos
- A website containing text, photos, and graphics
- An academic journal containing articles on a particular topic
- A newspaper comprised of articles by different journalists
- A catalog comprised of text and photographs

In the above examples, original authorship may be involved in deciding which were the best stories, the biggest hits, greatest photos, the appropriate article for the serial, and in what order to present the respective works within the compilation.

1.7. Basic Elements of Infringement

Copyright infringement may have one or more of the following basic elements like following:

i. Reproduction of the work

ii. Publication of the work

iii. Communication of the work to the public

iv. Making adaptations and translations of the work and doing any of the above acts in relation to a substantial part of the work.

v. Differences in dimension of contents or an inappropriate presentation of contents cannot help any publication from being infringed if a significant or considerable portion of the content has been copied. Direct evidences on copying are rarely available and this can be reasoned out by other corroborative evidences. Same errors, similarity in languages and peculiarity of writing style amount to enough evidences for copyright infringement.

Infringement can be primary and secondary as well. *Primary Infringement* occurs when a copyright owner's economic rights are violated or infringed. *Secondary infringement* occurs in few cases like,

(a) Importing infringing copy

(b) Possessing or dealing with infringing copy

(c) Provides means for making infringing copy

(d) Permitting use of premises for infringing performance

(e) Providing apparatus for infringing performance

1.8. Fair Dealing or Fair Use

There are certain circumstances where copyright is limited, other than just for duration or territory. Copyright can be limited where it serves a specific public interest, such as provided for by exceptions and limitations to copyright that conform to international treaties. For example, countries have "fair use" or "fair dealing" provisions enacted in their copyright laws that permit users in certain circumstances to use copyright-protected works without

prior authorization. Domestic laws have enacted exceptions to copyright protection for the preservation and management of cultural heritage patrimony, for example, or in the interests of serving the educational community. Fair use is the *balancing provisions* between the interest of copyright owners and creative interest of the society.

In the event that someone exercises the rights of a copyright owner without obtaining consent, then the rights of the copyright owner have been infringed. Unauthorized copying or distribution of copyright protected content is sometimes referred to as "piracy". Committing infringement can lead to civil damages, criminal liability or both. And, with the advent of the Internet and new technologies, piracy has become an issue at the forefront.

The doctrine of fair use or fair dealing has been detailed in Section 52 of Indian Copyright Act 1957. The moral justification of copyright is that a person should be able to reap the benefits of his creation or mechanical labour. On the other hand, the doctrine of fair use seeks to limit that exclusive right, to some extent, in specific instances of overriding social interest.

Section 52 (1) provides that a fair dealing with a literacy, dramatic, musical, or artistic work for the following purposes does not constitute infringement:

1. A fair dealing with a literacy, dramatic, musical or artistic work, not being a computer programme, for the purpose of private use including research, criticism or review, making copies of computer programme for certain purposes , reporting current events in newspapers and magazines or by broadcasting or in a cinematograph film or by means of photographs.
2. Reproduction for judicial proceedings and reports thereof, reproduction exclusively for the use of

members of legislature, reproduction (artistic work excluded) in a certified copy supplied in accordance with law.

3. Reading or recitation in public of extracts (literary or dramatic work).
4. Publication in a collection for the use of educational institutions in certain circumstances.
5. Reproduction by teacher or pupil in the course of instructions or in question papers.
6. Performance in the course of activities of educational institutions in certain circumstances.
7. The making of sound recording under certain circumstances subject to certain conditions.
8. The causing of a sound recording to be heard in public by utilizing it in an enclosed room or in clubs in certain circumstances.
9. Performance in an amateur club given to a non-paying audience or for religious institutions.
10. Reproduction in newspaper and magazine of an article on current economic, political, social or religious topics in certain circumstances.
11. Publication in newspapers or magazines a report of a lecture delivered in public.
12. Making a maximum of 3 copies for the use of a public library.
13. Reproduction of unpublished work kept in a museum or library for the purpose of study or research.
14. Reproduction or publication of any matter published in official Gazette or reports of Government Commission or other bodies appointed by Government.
15. Reproduction of any judgment or order of court, tribunal or other judicial authority not prohibited from publication.

16. Production or publication of translation of Acts of Legislature or Rules.
17. Making or publishing of a painting , drawing or photographs of a work of architecture.
18. Making or publishing of a painting , drawings or photographs or engraving of sculpture or other artistic work permanently situate in public place.
19. Inclusion in a cinematograph film of any artistic work permanently situate in a public place and other artistic work by way of background or incidental to the principal matter represented in the film.

Computer Programme [Section 52 (1) (aa)]

In respect of computer programme the following acts do not constitute infringement:

The making of copies or adaptation of a computer programme by the lawful possessor of a copy of such computer programme from such copy-

1. In order to utilize the computer programme for the purpose for which it was supplied; or
2. To make back-up copies purely as a temporary protection against loss, destruction or damage in order only to utilize the computer programme for the purpose for which it was supplied.

Examples of fair use

- Quotation of short passages in a scholarly or technical work for illustration or clarification of the author's observations.
- Spontaneous and unexpected reproduction of material for classroom use–for example, where an article in the morning's paper is directly relevant to that day's class topic.
- A parody that includes short portions of a work.
- A summary of an address or article, which may include quotations of short passages of the copyright-protected work.

2

Concept of Fair Use

Fair use is both an extraordinary opportunity and a source of recurring confusion. — **Kenneth D. Crews**

(*Renowned US Professor in Law, Library & Information Science and Business*)

2.0. Introduction

"*Ex nihilo*" is Latin word for "from nothing." The term "*creation ex nihilo*" refers to God creating everything from nothing. In the beginning, God created the heavens and the earth. Prior to that moment there was nothing. God didn't make the universe from preexisting building blocks. He started from scratch. But this creation has nothing to do with copyright act.

Humans can be very creative, but we require materials from which to build something. Fair use is the right to make a limited use of another's copyright, but prior to creation of the fair use doctrine, others had what was effectively an unlimited right to use another's work in a different form. A second author, for example, could abridge (or translate) the first author's work and thereby obtain his or her own copyright. For a second author to reap what he or she had not sown was deemed to be unfair, and courts limited the right to do so by the fair use doctrine.

2.1. History of Fair Use

Case of Folsom v. Marsh of 1841, a 19th-century US copyright case, is widely considered as the origin of fair use. The opinion was written by *Judge Joseph Story*, who set forth four factors that are in use today for fair use analysis.

The Reverend Charles Wentworth Upham, a writer and anthologist, had copied 353 pages from the plaintiff's 12-volume biography of George Washington published by Charles Folsom of Folsom in order to produce a separate two-volume work of his own published by Bela Marsh. He was sued for "piracy of the copyright". The defendant argued that the papers were not copyrightable because, as the letters of a deceased author, they were not private property and not "proper subjects of copyright"; that even if copyrightable, as works of the President they belonged to the United States; and lastly, that their use was fair, because it was the creation of an essentially new work.

The court in this case examined the justifiable use of original materials, forming the basis for the fair use doctrine. The court found that, "the question of piracy, often depend upon a nice balance of the comparative use made in one of the materials of the other; the nature, extent, and value of the materials thus used; the objects of each work; and the degree to which each writer may be fairly presumed to have resorted to the same common sources of information, or to have exercised the same common diligence in the selection and arrangement of the materials." Justice Story thus destroyed the "abridgment doctrine", while establishing what has come to be known as the "fair use" doctrine.

Over the next century and a half, *Folsom v. Marsh* was repeatedly cited for its discussion of what uses might be fair, leading to the establishment of what has come to be known as the fair use doctrine. This doctrine was ultimately incorporated into the Section 107 of 1976 US Copyright Act. This section includes the factors themselves are essentially the same as set forth by Judge Story in 1841. Consequently, the *Folsom v. Marsh* case is regarded as establishing the principle of fair use.

2.1.1. Theoretical Premise of Fair Use

Wilmer Hale Professor of Intellectual Property Law, Harvard University, William W. Fisher III proposed *Welfare Theory* as one of the four theories of copyright including *fairness theory, personality theory* and *culture theory* as constitutional basis for fair use. The *welfare theory* of copyright advocates the interests of society as a whole and promotes the greatest good for the greatest number of people. This system balances incentives to create with mechanisms to make works widely available for the benefit of the society.

2.2. Fair Dealing in India

Provisions of fair dealing was first enacted in 1914 in copyright act in India which was literally implemented Imperial Copyright Act of 1911 essentially a British law. It was mere a duplication of section 2 (1) (i) of the British Copyright Act, 1911. Present Indian Copyright Act of 1957, an independent and self-contained law also greatly borrowed from the UK Copyright Act of 1956. Section 52 deals with the fair dealing and now the scope of fair dealing has been increased than 1914 act. After 1957, it was amended thrice to add more subjects under the purview of this section 52.Fair dealing provision was amended in1983, 1994 and in 1999 respectively for the inclusion of private research, computer programming etc.

- Fair use is vital to the growth of knowledge.
- Fair use is based on a balancing of four factors set forth in the statute.
- Fair use can apply to a wide range of materials and activities.
- Fair use does not have defined boundaries, but is flexible for changing needs.
- Fair use ensures that copyrights are not overprotected; and that the law allows new creativity based on existing works.

- By Kenneth D. Crews

2.3. What is Fair Use?

Law provides copyright protection to creative works in order to foster the culture of creation. It's best known feature is protection of owners' rights. But copying, quoting, and generally re-using existing copyrighted material can be, under some circumstances, a critically important part of generating new knowledge and new creation. In fact, we as a society award limited property rights to creators to encourage them to produce creative works; at the same time, we allow other creators to use that same copyrighted material, without permission or payment, in some circumstances.

Kenneth D. Crews defined that *Fair use is an essential counterbalance to the widening range of rights that copyright law grants to owners. At various times, fair use has been called a right, a privilege, and a defense. Whatever the label, the doctrine is a legally sanctioned opportunity. It allows the public to make limited uses of copyrighted works-uses that might otherwise constitute infringement-specially for advancing knowledge or serving other important social objectives.*

Dan L. Burk & Julie E. Cohen described fair use as "*safety valve*" that mediates between the strictures of copyright and the creative demands of the society (*Burk & Cohen, 2001*).

New creation inevitably incorporates existing copyrighted material. As copyright protects more works for longer periods than ever before, creators face new challenges: licenses to incorporate copyrighted sources become more expensive and more difficult to obtain—and sometimes are simply unavailable. As a result, fair use has become more important today than ever before.

Fair use is flexible.
It is not uncertain
It is not unreliable.

2.4. Flexibility of Fair Use

Fair use is flexible; it is not unreliable. The copyright act has not specifically defined the term 'fair use'. This provides us an opportunity and poses confusion as well. In fact, for any particular field of critical or creative activity, lawyers and judges consider expectations and practice in assessing what is fair within that field.

Copyright law does not specify exactly how to apply fair use and that gives the fair use doctrine a flexibility that works to the advantage of users. Creative needs and practices differ with the field, with technology, and with time. Rather than following a specific formula, lawyers and judges decide whether an unlicensed use of copyrighted material is fair according to a "rule of reason." This means taking all the facts and circumstances into account to decide if an unlicensed use of copyrighted material generates social or cultural benefits that ultimately are greater than the costs it imposes on the copyright owner.

In any case, fair use is not medium specific. The principles of fair use apply equally to a university publication and to a Web site. However, since all fair use instances are context dependent and case-by-case, potential fair users of copyrighted material will weigh all the circumstances in making a decision about how to proceed.

Fair use is in wide and vigorous use today in many professional communities. For example, historians regularly quote both other historians' writings and primary textual sources; filmmakers and visual artists use, reinterpret, and critique copyrighted material; scholars illustrate cultural commentary with textual, visual, and musical examples. Equally important is the example of commercial news media. Fair use is healthy and vigorous in daily broadcast television news, where references to popular films, classic TV programs, archival images, and popular songs are both prevalent and routinely unlicensed.

For education and research, fair use is the most important exception to the the right of copyright owners, because it is flexible and adaptable to many unpredictable situations and needs that occur as we pursue diverse projects and apply innovative technologies in academia. Fair use can be applied to all types of media and all types of works. Flexibility is one of the prized virtues of fair use. It is also the source of perennial source of uncertainty and confusion. Copyright act has deliberately created a flexible fair use provisions that gives no exact parameters allowing fair use to take into account the circumstances of each case.

2.5. Determination of Fair Use- Four Factor Analysis

Objectives of Fair Use

1. Advancing social utility by increasing the supply of intellectual products and facilitating their distribution
2. Enforcing an author's natural right to a reasonable portion of the fruits of his labor;
3. Protecting an author's interest in controlling the way in which his creations are presented to the world; and finally
4. Aligning the law with custom and popular conceptions of decent behavior

Understanding the scope and concept of fair use is very important from librarians and educators point of view and becoming familiar with those situations where it is more likely to apply and those where it is less likely to—can help guard appropriate authority and their institution from an infringement claim due to the unauthorized use of copyright-protected materials.

The concept of "fair use" seems to be still dubious and not formulated at all. These days, interactive technologies' enormous power to copy, disseminate, manipulate electronic information makes even difficult to gauge the proper application of fair use in the marketplace.

There are no set guidelines that are universally accepted. But Section 107 of the US Copyright Act sets forth 4 factors to evaluate and balance for determination of fair use. Analysis of these 4 factors for determining 'fair dealing' provisions of Indian Copyright Act here in India will also be useful. The analysis of these four factors is popularly known as *PNAM test* (*taking first letter from most prominent term of each factor*) or *four factor analysis.*

1. the **P**urpose and character of the use,
2. the **N**ature of the copyrighted work;
3. the **A**mount and substantiality of the portion used
4. the effect of the use on the potential **M**arket for the copyrighted work

The purpose and character of the use **[Factor 1]**

- Is the new work merely a copy of the original? If it is simply a copy, it is not as likely to be considered fair use.
- Does the new work offer something above and beyond the original? Does it transform the original work in some way? If the work is altered significantly, used for another purpose, appeals to

a different audience, it more likely to be considered fair use.

- Is the use of the copyrighted work for nonprofit or educational purposes? The use of copyrighted works for nonprofit or educational purposes is more likely to be considered fair use.

The nature of the copyrighted work **[Factor 2]**

- Is the copyrighted work a published or unpublished works? Unpublished works are less likely to be considered fair use.
- Is the copyrighted work out of print? If it is, it is more likely to be considered fair use.
- Is the work factual or artistic? The more a work tends toward artistic expression, the less likely it will be considered fair use.

The amount and substantiality of the portion used **[Factor 3]**

- The more you use, the less likely it will be considered fair use.
- Does the amount you use exceed a reasonable expectation? If it approaches 50 percent of the entire work, it is likely to be considered an unfair use of the copyrighted work.
- Is the particular portion used likely to adversely affect the author's economic gain? If you use the "heart" or "essence" of a work, it is less likely your use will be considered fair.

The effect of use on the potential market for the copyrighted work **[Factor 4]**

- The more the new work differs from the original, the less likely it will be considered an infringement.
- Does the work appeal to the same audience as the original? If the answer is yes, it will likely be considered an infringement.

- Does the new work contain anything original? If it does, it is more likely the use of the copyrighted material will be seen as fair use.

Besides, various types and characteristics of information contents are also very important from the perspective of fair use.

2.5.1. Checklist for Fair use

Following checklist can be used by teachers, librarians, researchers, student, scholars or any stakeholder to determine the use of copyrighted materials is fair or not. This check list is a tool for practical purposes.

Directions : *Check all boxes that apply. For each of the four sections below, determine whether that factor favors or disfavors a finding of fair use. Where the factors favoring "fair use" outnumber the factors weighing against a finding of "fair use," reliance on the fair use exception is justified. Where less than half of the factors favor "fair use," permission should be obtained before copying or disseminating copies of the work.*

Name: ______________	Date ______________
Institution: ______________	Project ______________
Title of the Copyrighted Work ______________	
Portion to be used ______________	
[Factor 1] Favoring Fair Use	**Disfavoring Fair Use**
• Educational * Teaching (including multiple copies for classroom) * Research * Scholarship * Criticism * Comment * News reporting * Restricted access (ex-among students) • Transformative or Productive Use • Non-commercial use • Parody	• Commercial, entertainment or other • Non-transformative/Verbatim or exact copy • Commercial use * Entertainment * Profit • Unrestricted use • Reproductions

[Factor 2] Favoring Fair Use	**Disfavoring Fair Use**
• Published work • Factual or non-fiction based • Important to favored educational objectives	• Unpublished work • Creative expressions • Consumables (workbook, test etc.) • Unpublished
[Factor 3] Favoring Fair Use	**Disfavoring Fair Use**
• Small quantity • Portion is not heart of the work • Appropriate to educational purpose • Low resolution image	• Large quantity or entire work • Portion is the heart of the work • Inappropriate for educational purpose • High resolution image
[Factor 4] Favoring Fair Use	**Disfavoring Fair Use**
• No significant impact on market • No longer in print or absence of licensing mechanism • Few copied made or distributed • One time use or spontaneous use	• Significant impact on market • Print copy and licensing available • Numerous copies made or distributed • Long term or recurring use

2.5.2. Fair Use Classic Cases: International

Let us discuss few important classic international and national cases to grasp and to understand various interpretations to the concept of fair use.

Campbell V. Acuff-Rose Music, Inc (1994)

It is the cornerstone case of fair use. In 1994 the US Supreme Court decided the case *Campbell, V. Acuff-Rose Music, inc.* involving 2 Live Crew's rendition of the Roy Orbison song "Oh, Pretty Woman." In keeping with the general confusion that the courts have demonstrated regarding fair use, the district court granted summary judgment finding 2 Live Crew's version to be parody and the use fair. The Court of Appeals reversed this decision finding that because 2 Live Crew's song was a commercial undertaking, it was presumptively unfair. Finally, the Supreme Court sided with the district court's original judgment and found that parody, even in the context of a commercial undertaking- a *transformative, repurposed* from the original song and *does not compete for the market* with the original version, is a fair use.

The purpose of the original : To entertain general audience

The purpose of the new work : To criticize the original one

Mechanism : Transformation and repurposing with no significant market impact

Result : Fair use

Bill Graham Archives v. Dorling Kindersley (2006)

Bill Graham Archives vs. Dorling Kindersley, Ltd. (2006)

It's another classic case fair use of 2006. *Dorling Kindersley* ("DK") is a US publisher of popular books, including colorful picture books for children and "coffee table books". In October 2003, DK and Grateful Dead Productions published *Grateful Dead: The Illustrated Trip*. The book was a 480-page coffee table book that included a wide variety of Grateful Dead-related information and imagery. The book included a timeline "running continuously through the book, chronologically combining over 2000 images representing dates in the Grateful Dead's history with explanatory text.

The *Grateful Dead* were an American rock band formed in 1965 in Palo Alto, California. Ranging from quintet to septet, the band was known for its unique and eclectic style, which fused elements of country, folk, bluegrass, blues, reggae, rock, improvisational jazz, psychedelic, space rock, for live performances of lengthy instrumental jams, and for their devoted fan base, known as "Deadheads".

DK had sought permission from *Bill Graham Archives* ("BGA") for the use of seven images but after negotiations fell through used the images without permission. The seven images were originally Grateful Dead event posters, and they were reproduced as thumbnails or low resolution images along the timeline, along with captions describing the actual events.

DK declined to pay BGA's licensing demands after publication, and BGA sued. The District Court (SDNY) granted summary judgment to DK on their fair use defense. Bill Graham Archives appealed to the Second Circuit. DK, represented by copyright scholar William Patry, again asserted fair use, and the Second Circuit affirmed: "We agree with the district court that DK's use of the copyrighted images is protected as fair use.

The purpose of the original : To generate publicity for a concert.

The purpose of the new work : To document and illustrate the concert events in historical context.

Mechanism : Transformation and repurposing with no significant market impact

Result : Fair use

Roger V. Koons (1992)

Art Rogers, a 43-year-old professional artist-photographer, has a studio and home at Point Reyes, California, where he makes his living by creating, exhibiting, publishing and otherwise making use of his rights in his photographic works. In 1980 an acquaintance, Jim Scanlon, commissioned Rogers to photograph his eight new German shepherd puppies. When Rogers went to his home on September 21, 1980 he decided that taking a picture of the puppies alone would not work successfully, and chose instead to include Scanlon and his wife holding them. Substantial creative effort went into both the composition and production of "Puppies," a black and white photograph. At the photo session, and later in his lab, Rogers drew on his years of artistic development. He selected the light, the location, the bench on which the Scanlons are seated and the arrangement of the small dogs. He also made creative judgments concerning technical matters with his camera and the use of natural light. He prepared a set of "contact sheets," containing 50 different images, from which one was selected.

Art Rogers took the original photo of a couple holding puppies and used it on greeting cards. Its adorable, but perhaps bland. Artist Jeff Koons hired sculptors to create the sculpture on the right, and directed them to closely copying the details of the photo. Koons displayed the sculpture in his "banality" exhibit in 1988, and sold 3 copies for a total of $376,000.

The Koons sculpture was not fair use because it

was (1)(a) made for a commercial purpose; (1)(b) not a parody because it did not comment on the original (2) the original Rogers work was artistic rather than factual; (3) Koons copied nearly all of the original Rogers photo; and (4) the Koons sculpture diminished the value of Rogers' photos:

The purpose of the original : Artistic creation

The purpose of the new work : Commercial sculpture based on the original work

Mechanism : Copying from the original work

Result : Not Fair Use

Suntrust Bank v. Houghton Mifflin (2001)

The Wind Done Gone (TWDG), a book was written by Alice Randall published by Houghton Mifflin Co. of the USA just jumbling of words of the title of the classic novel *Gone With the Wind* (GWTW) written by Margaret Mitchell. A copyright infringement case was sued by the estate of Margaret Michell against TWDG but the court upheld the plea for fair use advocated by it in the defense of the suit. TWDG borrowed 18 characters from GWTW made in the backdrop of *American Civil War* and *Reconstruction,* made only transparent changes in the character names, and for much of the book recounted many of the same incidents—but altogether altered the virtues and vices of the white and the black characters, and made concomitant alterations in the story line.

The purpose of the original : To narrate historical facts *of American Civil War* and *Reconstruction*

The purpose of the new work : To the institutions and values romanticized in GWTW are exposed as corrupt and made a parody over it

Mechanism : Parody in the sense of critical commentary

Result : Fair use

Batlin & Son, Inc. v. Snyder (1976)

A long time ago, a manufacturer produced some metal piggy banks that had the character of Uncle Sam on them. They were popular for a while, but the manufacturer eventually stopped production and the design fell in the public domain.

Years later, a toymaker named Snyder produced a plastic version of the Uncle Sam bank. It had slight design changes, and was made of plastic instead of metal, but it was very similar. Snyder registered a copyright of his design.

Batlin was a competitor. He produced metal Uncle

Sam banks that were similar to both Snyder's version and the original version. Snyder told Batlin to stop violating his copyright, and Batlin sued to have Snyder's copyright declared invalid.

Batlin argued that Snyder couldn't copyright the design because it was too derivative of the public domain original.

Snyder argued that his bank was sufficiently different from the public domain original to be copyrightable, and that Batlin's version was sufficiently similar to his to be a copyright infringement.

Although there were some design variations between Snyder's plastic bank and the public domain version, the court found them to be trivial, not readily discernible, and largely dictated by the mechanical needs of the plastic-molding process.

The purpose of the original : Artistic creation used commercially

The purpose of the new work : Commercial derivative work based on the original work having trivial changes.

Mechanism : Copying from the original work

Result : Not Fair Use

Harry Potter and Saga of Cases

Any commercially successful book attracts many seeking free riders to creative output of others. The success of Harry Potter written by J. K. Rowling is not unknown to anyone. The first six books sold over 325 million copies worldwide. It is translated in 65 languages. Five Hollywood film adaptations of this book by Warner Bros, who have the film rights have earned US$4 billion from ticket sales only. The infringement ranges from scanned the whole book and distributed online to selling in e-Bay. It has also spawned a range derivative and transformative works –some were not recognized as parody and some were able to get status as parody of the original.

Tanya Grotter – a female analogous of Harry Potter written in a series by a Russian Author Dmitry Yemets. This central character has close resemblance with Harry Potter. Owing to this resemblance, J K Rowling and her publishers brought a successful legal action in the Dutch courts in 2003 to prevent the distribution outside Russia of a Dutch translation of *Tanya Grotter and the Magical Double Bass*. The Dutch courts rejected the arguments put forward by Mr. Yemets and his Moscow-based publishers, who claimed that the books constituted a parody, permissible under copyright law exemptions.

A number of Harry Potter parodies are however in circulation have not faced any legal sanction yet. One of those is *Barry Trotter and the Shameless Parody.* It is a series of Harry Potter parodies written by Michael Gerber and published in the UK in a small hardback format which has been sold over 700,000 copies.

2.5.2. Fair Dealing Classic Cases: National

Blackwood and Sons Ltd. and Ors. Vs A.N. Parasuraman and Ors. on 28 February, 1958 (Madras High Court)

The Complaint of Plaintiffs

The plaintiff, Messrs. Macmillan and Co. Ltd. brought a legal suit against the defendants "The Little Flower and Co.", Madras based publishing house. The plaintiffs claimed that they were assignee of two works (1) *The Return of the Native by Thomas Hardy,* and (2) A collection of stories by Rabindranath Tagore published under the style of "*Stories from Tagore*". The first book was prescribed by the University of Madras for the B. A. degree examination 1956, Part I English.

Second book was prescribes as text book for the Intermediate Examination of the University of Madras also of 1956 for Part I English.

The defendants published in 1954 in Madras two guidebooks on the original texts. The primary complaint of the plaintiff was that these two "guides" reproduced substantial parts of the two original works and that though called "guide" they were in reality copies of the original works which competed with their books and market of these two books have been affected.

Relief Claimed

The relief claimed by the plaintiffs were disclosure of sales account arising out of the sales of these two guides, immediate injunctions of restraining the defendants from printing, publishing or selling of the books complained of or other editions thereof and directing the defendants to pay damages and render an account of the profits arising out of the defendants' publications and also the delivery to the plaintiffs of copies of the guides which were now in the defendants possession.

Pleas of Defendants

The defendants denied infringement by stating that their guide did not contain the reproduction of any substantial part of Hardy's novel. They also pleaded that in any event, their guide was "a fair dealing". In regard to "Stories from Tagore", that the Stories from Tagore included in the plaintiffs' volume were first written and published in Bengali by Rabindranath Tagore and that they were not translated into English therefore, urged that there was no copyright in the said translations.

Final Judgement

Fair dealing claimed by the defendants for the purpose of private study of their published guides of the plaintiff's books was fully rejected by the Madras High Court. It was held that private study covers the student copying the book for his own use, and not circulation of copies among other students. It gave a restricted meaning of 'private study'.

The court also held that translation of an original work is copyrightable subject provided the translator has invested his intellectual labor in terms of application adequate effort and skill for the work.

Syndicate Press of University of Cambridge v. Kasturi Lal & Sons, on 31 May, 2005 (Delhi High Court)

The Complaint of Plaintiffs

The plaintiff, the Syndicate Press (the trade name of Cambridge University Press), is the sole copyright owner of the book-"*Advanced Grammar in Use by Martin Hewings*". This book is low priced Indian edition (priced at only $ 2 or Rs. 95 instead of international price $ 29.00) has been prescribed and used in several institutions and universities all over the world and including Guru Nanak Dev University, Amritsar ('GNDU') in the State of Punjab for the students of Bachelor of Arts Part I, II and III commencing for the year 2004-05.

The defendant, Kasturi Lal & Sons (KLS) had published three guide books, for the original text book published by the Syndicate Press namely, "KLS A Text Book of General English for B.A./B.Sc./B.Com. Part-I (G.N.D.U.)", "KLS A Text Book of General English for B.A./ B.Sc./B.Com. Part-II (G.N.D.U and "KLS A Text Book of General English for B.A./B.Sc./B.Com. Part-III (G.N.D.U.)". The plaintiff complained that the defendants guidebooks are mere copy of the original book including verbatim, exercises and answer keys to the exercises.

Pleas of Defendants

The defendants, KLS pleaded that they were the approved publisher of prescribed books of GNDU and they published guidebooks to elucidate and clarify the subjects predominantly for the rural students.

Final Judgement

The court found that defendants work is simply a copy and merely reproduced from the original one by mechanical manner. The defendant's claim for 'fair dealing' under section 52 was standstill rejected by the Delhi High Court. The Delhi High Court observed that:

"Law should encourage enterprise, research and scholarship but such encouragement cannot come at the cost of the right of an individual to protect against the misappropriation of what is essentially a product of his intellect and ingenuity. The law encourages innovation and improvement but not plagiarism. Copyright is a form of protection and not a barrier against research and scholarship. Lifting portions of the original work and presenting it as one's own creation can in no way be described as any form of bona fide enterprise or activity. Research and scholarship are easily distinguishable from imitation and plagiarism."

Harry Potter Vs Hari Puttar

The Complaint of Plaintiffs

Hari Puttar is a 2008 Indian family drama film directed by Lucky Kohli and Rajesh Bajaj. Warner Bros, the multinational entertainment company filed a lawsuit against production company Mirchi Movies to stop the release of the film due to the similarity of its title to that of the *Harry Potter* film series. Primary complaint was that the Punjabi comedy, of which producers was "guilty of infringing the Warner Brothers trademarks" for choosing to name their movie Hari Puttar—a name "visually and phonetically similar to Harry Potter."

Pleas of Defendants

Mirchi Movies Chief Executive Officer (CEO) Munish Purii insisted that there was very little similarity between *Hari Puttar* and any elements in the *Harry Potter* franchise, and explained that Hari is a popular Indian name, while "puttar" means "son" in the Punjabi language.

Final Judgment

Delhi High Court says Harry Potter and Hari Puttar are like chalk and cheese. "To put it differently," said the court, "*the possibility of an unlettered audience viewing a Harry Potter movie is remote, to say the least. An illiterate or semi-literate movie viewer, in case he ventures to see a film by the name of Hari Puttar, would never be able to relate the same with a Harry Potter film or book.*" Justice Khetrapal said "*Harry Potter*" *was neither a "soap or a pharmaceutical product" to be mistakenly picked up by an unwary buyer. The Potter chronicles caters to an "educated person who has pored over the stories.*" With this, the Delhi High Court finally dismissed the challenge thrown by Warner Brothers against the title of the Punjabi comedy Hari Puttar—A Comedy of Terrors (*Rajagopal 2008*).

2.6. Fair Dealing Vs Fair Use

I opine that out of these two approaches, however context dependent, 'Fair Use' provision as enacted in Section 107 of the 1976 US Copyright Act is superior to 'Fair Dealings' provision as enacted in Section 52 of the Indian Copyright Act. This is primarily because of the following:

1. The Indian laws related to 'fair dealing' is always considered rigid and conventional as it provides an exhaustive list and any use falling out of the statutory list is considered as an act of infringement. Indian law has adopted enumerated exception approach whereas US has adopted open ended approach. Scope of US fair use is much wider and broader than Indian fair dealing.
2. Indian laws of fair dealing work strictly within the framework of the enlisted actions which constitute fair dealing, the American laws of fair use is open for interpretation and works with the help of only certain guideline factors which help in determining the extent of "fairness" involved in the work.
3. Fair use provision can be applied to any works but fair dealing is restricted to literary, dramatic, musical and artistic works.
4. In US system, fair use is a right that is protected by the First Amendment of US Constitution. In India, it is not clear whether fair dealing will be classified as a defense or a user right. Section 52 of the Indian Copyright Act uses the words: "*The following acts shall not constitute an infringement of copyright, namely:...*" Based on this language, it could be argued that the fair dealing provisions under the Indian Copyright Act are not a right but a defense or an exception (*Matthan R., & Narendran N. , 2011*).
5. Section 107 explicitly mentioned 4 factors for

determining of fair use which are absent in Indian law. Use of these 4 factors-namely purpose of the use, nature of the use, amount of the use and impact on the potential market are very scientific and logical. There is no scope of any such analysis in Indian laws.

6. Fair use system of US is an example of legal norms not as a standard but fair dealing of India which has adopted enumerated exceptions as legal norms almost as a rule.
7. Fundamentally, US law has identified 4 factors for fair use which need to be considered by the judges while resolving any dispute, but it never tells judges why these factors are important. This reflects the substantive goal of US copyright system what it seeks to achieve like maximising social welfare, fair creation, protecting personhood interest and many such aspirations. But approach of Indian law lacks all those perspectives and rationalisation (*Fisher, W., 2015*).

2.7. Algorithm of Fair Use

One can use the following algorithm (Fig. 2) to ascertain his uses fair or not fair use of the copyrighted works.

Nature/type of Information

The nature of information is so important in deciding whether it is or not for fair use. Accordingly if copying of information is for advancing social utility such as education or pure academic research for public interest, it is more likely to fall into the area of fair use than copying for commercial use. Types of information (entertainment/ educational, commercial/non-commercial) is also useful to assess the appropriateness of fair use.

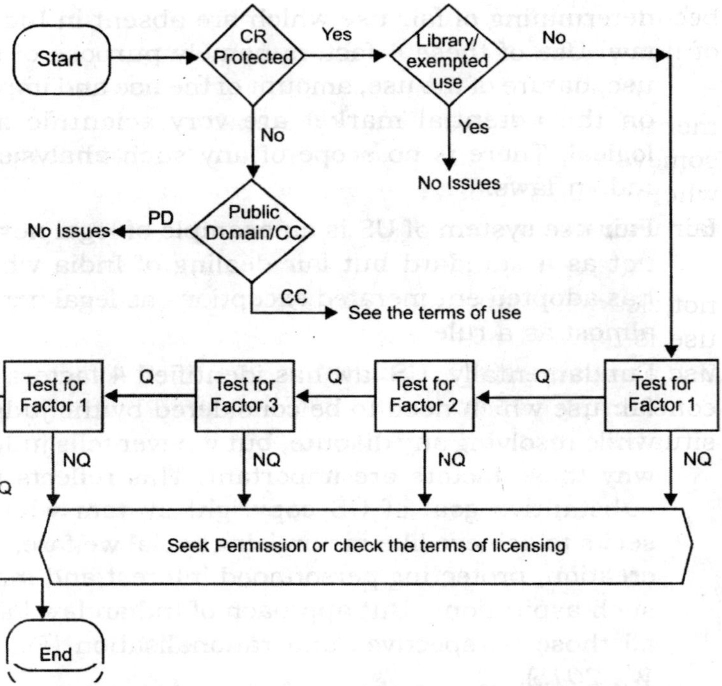

Fig. 2. Flow chart for determination of fair use CR-Copyright; CC-Creative Commons; PD –Public Domain; Q-Qualified; NQ-Non-qualified

Characteristics of Information Goods

Information is basically public goods. Therefore it has the characteristics of non-excludability (in consumption) and non-rivalry (in terms of utility). Accordingly copyright law forbidding users from unauthorized copying of intellectual products can be interpreted as a mechanism to eliminate the source of economic inefficiency by reviving excludability in information market. In a pay-per-use world, fair use rarely works, for pay-per-use could be carried to an extreme in which all electronic access and use require permission and/or payment.

However, if information is sold to each individual, it

becomes private goods though it still has a characteristic of non-rivalry.

A combination of information type and previously mentioned four factors for fair use allows us to have somewhat clear and predictable interpretation in deciding whether copying behavior without permission falls in the fair use domain or not.

While these four factors are helpful guides, they do not clearly identify uses that are or are not fair use. Fair use is not a straightforward concept; therefore, any fair use analysis must be conducted on a case-by-case basis considering all four factors and the circumstances of the situation at hand (*Yoo Euisn, 2000*).

3

Copyright and Universities

The dogmas of the quiet past are inadequate to the story present. The occasion is piled high with difficulty, and we must rise to the occasion. As our case is new, so we must think anew and act anew.

— Sir Abraham Lincoln (July 2, 1862)

3.0. Introduction

A primary mission of the University community is the exchange and development of ideas and information. Discovery, learning, and societal engagement are mutually supportive core missions of any research university around the world. They bring us into daily contact with the expressions of creative and innovative ideas embodied in print media, audio and video media, and computer media, among others. Universities are the producers as well as consumers of such expressions. Transfer of knowledge to those in society who can make use of it for the general good contributes to each of these missions. Many of the works containing these ideas are copyright protected and the consequences of infringement can be quite serious, therefore, an understanding of the impact of the copyright laws on our ability to utilize these works is very important.

The copyright law is intended to increase the free flow of ideas in order to further progress in science and the arts. This is the promotional tool for effective fostering of creative and innovative academic scholarship. Implementation of copyright law requires balancing the incentives given to authors to create works (the exclusive rights of reproduction, distribution, performance, etc.) against free access of others to the ideas contained in those works.

It is easy to imagine that a system seriously out of balance either way would hurt progress in science and the arts; no protection for authors might mean that fewer would be willing to invest the time and energy to create works; total control for authors or publishers over their works might severely restrict the public's use of the ideas contained in the works to develop new or derivative works or ideas.

"Fair use" is the concept that provides balance between the two extremes. There is much debate about what fair use is and what is not. Ultimately, fair use is what the courts decide it is on a case-by-case basis, taking into account all of the facts in a particular case.

Changing Scenario

The most important aspect of the present changing scenario is unpredictability. Educated people and their creation and ideas have become today's main asset of the society. Universities has never been so important than today. Knowledge we generate in the university are translated into personal as well as societal economic benefits and these are important in every contemporary society. New technological milieu and mass adoption has brought new opportunities as well as risk of misappropriation. Universities are built on public money and knowledge generates here is everybody's stake in our society. Complex media and formats have fostered uncertainties in assigning rights over the creative works and its reproduction, storage and distribution. Besides multi rights over a single work have made the situation worsen. Intensified market drove the universities, a public institution, towards a mere supplier of content industries like big academic publishing houses. Government funded research output are being published in subscription based scholarly journal just to elevate authors so-called reputation is very much counterproductive and self detrimental for the advancement of learning and promotion of scholarship.

The world of creativity and copyright ownership is facing uncertainties. This is a recent development. Earlier teachers could own their rights over their lectures and creative works made during the teaching-learning process as a sign of academic freedom. But now universities decide how much rights will be kept with the universities and how much will be distributed to the scholar and teacher creators based on emerging new techno-legal regimes.

3.1. University as an Information System

Universities have centuries of tradition surrounding a complex social structure of faculty, administrators, staff, and students. Universities also have specific objectives of teaching, research, and service, even, though each member of that social structure may have a different understanding of –or responsibility for-fulfilling those objectives. Yet these institutions are in no way monolithic. They are instead collection of individuals with often divergent interests, activities and pursuits. Faculties engage in teaching, research, and service; students attend to their studies and projects; administrators are responsible for the effective functioning of the university; and staff employees support the goals of their particular departments, agencies, or superiors. Exacerbating the complexity, universities are deeply affected by an environment comprising the general public, donors, lawmakers, and material suppliers, an all others who provide or utilize the university's resources.

To bring some structure to this disarray, a university may be perceived as a 'system' (*fig. 3 & fig. 4*) that utilizes certain 'inputs' in order to achieve particular 'outputs'. Inputs embrace all the essential ingredients of a functional university, including students, faculty, libraries, classrooms, and money. 'Outputs' are the products of those processes. Ideal outputs include educated students and new research findings. Because of the central significance of information processing in higher education, universities may be understood as specialized 'information systems'. Thus, 'inputs' include diverse information resources, such as books, journals, videos, and software. 'Outputs' may include new publications and better educated citizens through a fuller exposure to valuable information. Added to this system are 'processes' which range from simply reading the input materials to duplicating them for distribution. 'Feedback' allows the outputs to be evaluated in light of objectives from other system elements. To best serve the academic mission, each component should bolster the advancement and dissemination of knowledge.

Two other aspects of a system are imperative here. First, processes are often regulated by a variety of controls, particularly by policies that direct or restrict certain activities. These policies and other controls should ultimately serve the system's general objectives. Second, the effectiveness of a system and each component – including policies –can be evaluated only in environmental context. The entire system is set within an immediate environment shaped by the university's social mission to advance and disseminate knowledge; the quality of a copyright policy must be measured by its response to that mission. But universities are also surrounded by another environment comprising the rights of copyright owners to restrict some uses. The effectiveness of copyright policies must be judged in light of those demands as well.

These two basic environmental forces can be in direct conflict with one another. In specific, publishers and copyright owners exert pressure on universities, sometimes threatening liability. In addition, the public and academic community –including faculty, students, and university employees themselves –look to universities for education, research, and the advancement of knowledge. Demands conflict when academic pursuits require uses of materials that overlap with copyright owners and users diverge on their legal interpretations. Organizations must undertake a goal- setting process to resolve such conflicts, and policies can manifest that resolution and articulate relationship between environmental demands and organizational objectives.

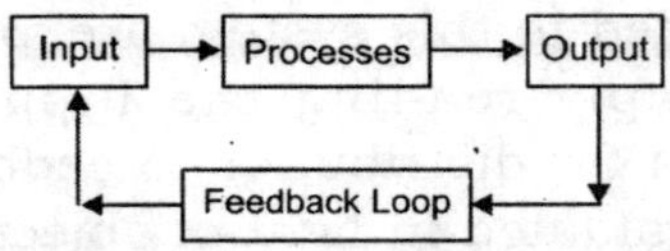

Fig. 3. Basic system structure (Source: *Kenneth D. Crews*)

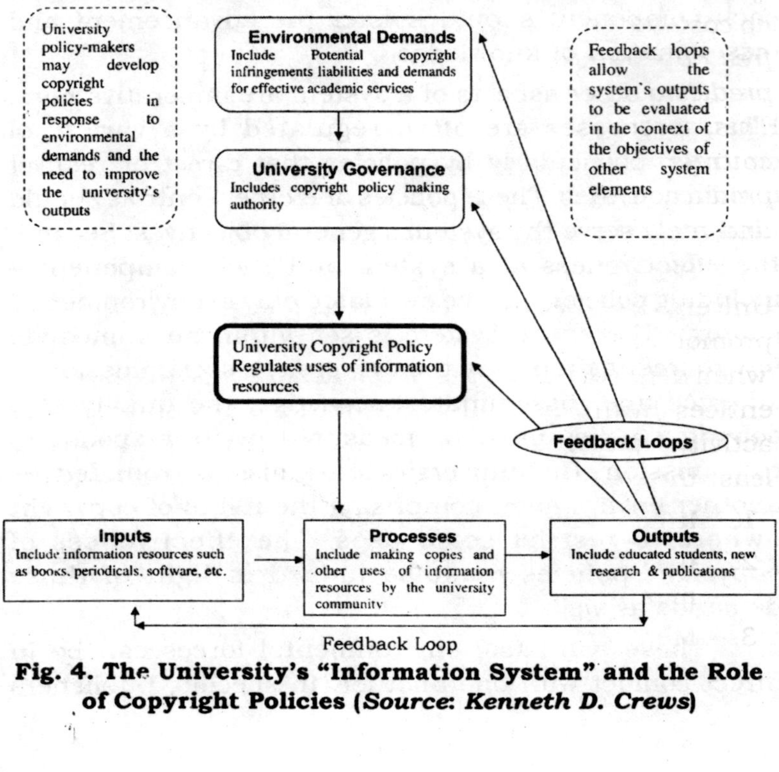

Fig. 4. The University's "Information System" and the Role of Copyright Policies (*Source*: *Kenneth D. Crews*)

3.1.1. Copyright Ownership in Universities

Copyright ownership in the university is a complicated issue. It is most often confusing and misunderstood laws affecting teaching-learning in universities. Copyright act is the reflection and response of different stakeholders' interest. Some complain that it is highly market-driven and commercialized that may not commensurate with its societal goal. Contrarily, economists consider intellectual property is a public good. Uma Suthersanen, Senior Fellow, Queen Mary Intellectual Property Research Institute, London opines *Public goods are non-excludable in that one cannot practically exclude people from using them, and they encourage non-rivalrous consumption in that the use of the good by one does not limit or leave less for the other to use. The problem with a public good is that if it is only regulated by the exigencies of market forces, the result is the obtaining of a benefit at no cost: i.e. free-riding. Due to the unavoidable presence of free riders, creation and dissemination of public goods is predicted to be lower than would be optimally efficient. This, we are told, is an instance of market failure. To counteract this market failure and ensure a steady production of public goods, state intervention is justified and required.*

Scholarship and learning has close relationships. Universities stand for the advancement of learning and promotion of scholarship. Boyer (1990, p.23) argues that 'when defined as *scholarship*...teaching both educates and entices future scholars'. Scholarship is defined as an activity that becomes scholarship when it possesses at least three attributes (*Shulman and Hutchings, 1998*):

1. It becomes public
2. It is subject to critical review and evaluation by members of one's community
3. Members of one's community begin to use, build upon and develop the activity.

An important fourth dimension of teaching scholarship is the posing of questions around issues of student learning (*Braxton et al., 2002*).

All scholarly activities in universities greatly produce new knowledge in any field of inquiry and discipline and it consumes by the society including the stakeholders in universities to generate further knowledge. Process continues indefinitely. It is knowledge cycle. Production of knowledge as well as consumption of knowledge both are subjected to copyright act. Creative output must be protected by the appropriate copyright act in order to make it a perennial process otherwise free riders will destroy the basic spirit of copyright protection and motivation of creativity will be dried up

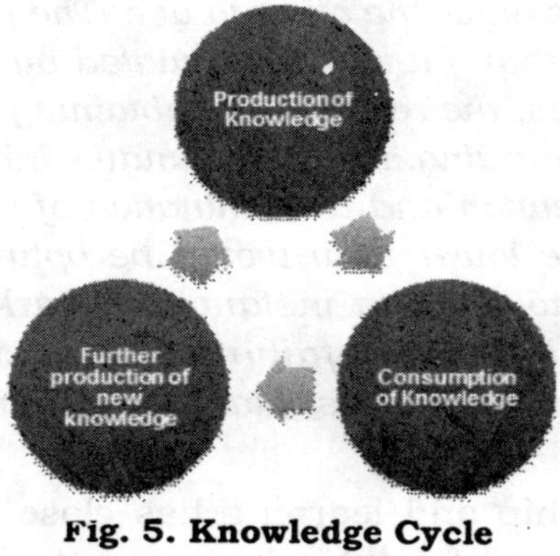

Fig. 5. Knowledge Cycle

Scholarship and Internet

Internet has emerged as a revolutionary tool as well as a mean that gradually rewritten and redefined the history of human scholarship into two distinct phases before internet era and after internet era. Research is considered as the most important component of scholarship. Over the years, most countries have defined the functions of higher education institutions and the roles of academics in terms of their three-fold responsibilities: teaching, research and scholarship, and service.

Scholarship before Internet

In earlier times, scholarship means a variety of creative works and its quality used to be judged by the ability to think, communicate and learn. The word 'research' is of recent origin and was first used in England in 1870 and later introduced in US in 1907. Presently we use scholarly activity in relation with some research works done by the academics in colleges and universities and its subsequent publication. The mission of scholarship is glued with mission of higher education and universities. No doubt, scholarship means research activities but it also aims to define the term professoriate which seeks to communicate knowledge to students connecting with the higher aim of scholarship and universities. Varies from country to country, scholarship is primarily manifested through his publications in some tangible mediums that can be in the form of books, monograph, research articles, lecture notes, drawings, diagrams etc. Questions of copyright ownership, prior to the internet, were generally limited to discussions zeroing on the unauthorized publication of the copyrighted materials. After the enactment of the first copyright act in England, *the Statute of Anne* in 1710, the creators or authors were protected by the state by the copyright acts and the copyright owners had exclusive rights over their creations and could exclude others like right to reproduction, distribution, adaptation, publicly displaying or publicly performing within the limit of fair use. Historically, teachers' exception is given by the law which has been adopted in the act in name of fair dealing or fair use. With the advent of computer, internet and tremendous growth and its access to information and communication technology (ICT) particularly in the last three decades, the whole scenario of scholarship and copyright issues have become too blurred and complex. Present situation demands regular amendment of concerned sections and articles of the copyright act to embrace the digital culture prevailing in the society.

Scholarship after Internet

Now consider a situation sitting in home, office or while moving by car or bus you can access to content of a digital library or you can have access to the global knowledge sitting in any corner of the globe instead of searching and manually picking books from the stacks of a traditional library. With the inception of internet, world has changed the way it used to exist.

Birth of internet in 1969 by ARPANET (Advanced Research Project Agency Network-a project of the United States Department of Defense) has bifurcated the globe into two distinct eras. It has changed the way we think, the way we act, the way we create, the way we publish, the way we distribute and the way we access. Creation of new works certainly depends on the earlier published works or certain elements of pre-existing works are important for the advancement of scholarship.

In fact, nothing has changed in so called digital era except form and formats of the content, access method and its distribution. However, copyright laws equally applicable for digital contents but access management, plethora of complex permission and licensing, identification of rights owner in digital environment and enforcing the right have remarkably influenced scholarship in internet era.

Now access to the internet is indispensible part of a student to a scholar. Besides, the evolution of technologies for hardware, storage, networking as well as software constantly influencing and creating a new ambience for never before opportunities for scholarship. Size and shape of the devices are also evolving from standalone , laptop, tablet, to latest Smartphone have crucial roles in formulating and navigating the scholarship process.

Borgman, Christine L. (2010) explained 4 things that are core to digital scholarship like the *Internet, the World Wide Web (WWW), the Computer Grid and the Digital*

Library. Though sometimes, internet and www are conflated but the www basically a specific application for accessing digital contents in linked environment. It was invented in CERN (European Organization for Nuclear Research), Geneva by Sir Timothy John Berners-Lee.

In a common sense, computer grid is analogous to electrical power grid that gives pervasive access to electricity. Like internet is as the network of networks, grid can also be said as the grid of grids. Thus each community of users have their own grids consist of interacting grids of science, social science, humanities etc for research and higher education.

Digital library as defined by the Father of the Green Stone Digital Library (GSDL) software, Prof. Ian Witten has clearly showed its role in scholarship. He defined digital library as-*a focused collection of digital objects, including text, video, and audio along with methods for access and retrieval, and for selection, organization, and maintenance of the collection*. He interpreted digital objects as 3D objects, simulations, dynamic visualizations and virtual reality.

For scholarship, communication plays a pivotal role across the continents. Digital content is fluid where content has liberated from its medium and malleable to store into an optical disk like CD or DVD or in any flash drive like pen drive or it can be stored in cloud by distributed computing. It can also be distributed over the internet as streaming content at the user end. It is observed that, connectivity is important for accessing digital content, but I opine that, better bandwidth is far more important than connectivity itself. Without adequate bandwidth content may not be accessed at all at the receiver end.

Access to scholarly digital content may be denied or may be partly accessed or accessed for a little period of time based on different licensing adopted to ensure copyright protection of the creators by using variants of Digital Rights Management (DRM) software. This discriminated access to the content has created some kind of digital divides worldwide.

More and more research organizations all over the world are also joining hands for better access to the scholarly contents by embracing and adopting open access as the guiding philosophy. Open access journals and a number of institutional repositories of universities and research organizations and laboratories have subscribed to this philosophy very actively, It has long term impact in the promotion of higher education, research and scholarship in developing nations like India.

In addition to it, social media platforms like ResearchGate, Academia.edu where researchers, professors and other similar stakeholders are regularly sharing their research papers, research findings firmly contributing their scholarly content to the world of scholarship in internet era.

3.2. Copyright Conflict & Photocopying

A Photocopy Center is a University facility that accommodates the needs of faculty and students for reasonably priced copies of materials that are required reading. Faculty members generally submit their required reading lists, i.e., chapters, articles, or excerpts from books and other publications, and the Copy Center prepares "packets" that contain these materials and makes them available to students. The charge for these packets is based upon the cost of preparation, including overhead, without any profit.

Ordinarily, copying printed material without the permission of the copyright owner is a violation of the rights of the copyright owners. Educational institutions have long relied upon the "fair use" exception of the copyright laws for protections from liability for the copying activities of photocopy Centers.

3.2.1. Classical Case of Kinko's in the USA

Kinko's (name of a photocopy company) operates a chain of copy centers all over the United States, usually located near universities and colleges. The practice the publishers complained of was Kinko's preparation of collections of excerpts from copyrighted books at the request of faculty at the nearby campuses. Kinko's copied the excerpts, assembled them into "course packets," and sold them to the students in the requesting faculty's class at a price that included a reasonable profit. Kinko's did not seek or obtain permission to copy any of the copyrighted material.

Kinko's defended the practice as, among other things, a fair use. The court analyzed Kinko's copying under Section 107 and under the Guidelines and concluded that the use was not fair, enjoined Kinko's from continuing the practice, and ordered Kinko's to pay $510,000 in statutory damages and attorney's fees and costs. The parties settled the litigation without appeal; Kinko's ultimately paid the publishers $1,875,000.

3.2.2. Case Two: Allowing Photocopy for students in Costa Rica

After thousands of Costa Rican students gathered outside the legislature to oppose a law that could make it illegal to photocopy extracts from textbooks, the President of Costa Rica decided to clear the air with a presidential decree clarifying the exception extended to photocopying academic material - - even if the photocopy shop makes a profit.

3.2.3. Case Three: Landmark Judgement on Photocopying of students in the University of Delhi

The petition was filed by three publishers—*Oxford University Press, Cambridge University Press and Taylor & Francis* —against *the University of Delhi* and *Rameshwari Photocopy Services*, alleged to have violated India's copyright law by selling photocopied compilations of study material as 'course packs'. The petitioners argue that this amounts to a parallel publishing enterprise of sorts that is not just illegal, but also harms their market sales. While the court has so far only ordered a seizure of all such course packs in stock on the shop's premises, the lawsuit claims damages of Rs 60 lakh as well.

Importantly, this is a photocopying vendor that has been selected by the university after floating a tender. In the interests of caution, a *license agreement* was drawn up containing strict *guidelines* - only *bonafide* students and faculty of the University could use the services and a uniform rate of 40 paisa per page could be charged which had to cover their equipment, labour and other operational costs.

Despite this, *the University of Delhi* and Rameshwari Photocopy Service have been restrained from photocopying extracts and compiling them into course packs for students. The injunction order has been passed by the Delhi High Court in September 2012.

In the Indian scenario, the law provisions are fairly straightforward – Photocopying extracts is legal under Section 52(1)(a) of the Indian Copyright Act that permits 'fair dealing for private use, including research' and 52(1)(i) that allows 'reproduction in the course of instruction by a teacher or pupil'. Unfortunately, the *injunction order* passed by the Delhi High Court was based on an *alleged 'admission', which was in fact a good faith defence* by the University under Section 76 of the Copyright Act.

The production of course packs in India, although perceived to be an unregulated practice, is actually a systematic method of furthering instruction by teachers, especially considering the high costs, limited copies with libraries and frequent unavailability of textbooks in India. This is clearly demonstrated by the license agreement between Rameswhari Photocopy Service and *the University of Delhi* where *strict guidelines* have been prescribed to ensure it is for *bonafide* uses and for students and faculty only.

More importantly, the photocopy shop here is only an extension of *the University of Delhi* and Ratan Tata Library and is even located within the university campus. They receive instructions from the Department on what exactly to photocopy, based on reading lists made available by professors and are barred from undertaking any 'outside jobs'. There is a formalized license agreement, with rules and guidelines, including the price that must be charged.

The above factors are also what distinguish Rameshwari from Kinkos and other commercial photocopy shops that also produce course packs and have been held by American courts to be commercial enterprises.

The course packs mentioned in the *University of Delhi* case do not reproduce an entire book even in a single case. In fact, a majority of the reproduction is well below the fair use threshold of 10% (a minimum of 3.5%). However, this figure of 10% itself must be challenged keeping in mind India's unique socio-economic conditions and the fact that access to knowledge is much easier in the U.S. compared to India (*Bansal 2012*).

Finally, Delhi High Court on 16th September 2016 in a landmark judgement rejected the plea placed by a group of publishers including *Oxford University Press, Cambridge University Press and Taylor & Franci*s and said that "Copyright is not a divine right". Copyright is there to promote creativity but not to impede the knowledge harvesting by the students. Thus labeling making photocopies by students out of their textbooks taken out from the library is not crime rather it should be considered as a process of knowledge harvesting by the students who otherwise cannot afford costly textbook. It also comes under the ambit of Section 52 of the Indian Copyright Act meant for fair dealing of the copyrighted works of creators.

Justice Rajiv Sahai Endlaw held that the act of students getting books copied from DU's library or its authorised photocopy shop enjoys protection under Section 52 of the Copyright Act, which exempts education from copyright infringement.

In a 94-page order, the court essentially concluded that if *the University of Delhi* can photocopy content within its library to impart education to students, then similar protection is enjoyed by the contractor, Rameshwari Photocopy Service (*Garg 2016*).

3.2.4. Case Four: Around the world

There have been decisions from across the world, holding the making and distribution of course packs for a non-commercial, educational purpose to be completely legal, with no need for a license. In a *decision* delivered recently, the Supreme Court of Canada held that the use of course packs by students' falls within the definition of 'private study or research'. Further, 'private' does not mean studying in isolation, but includes the classroom as well. The Court also determined that 'instruction' (found in India in Section 52(1)(i)) and 'research and private study' (found in S.52(1)(a)) were in fact a unified purpose since the purpose of the copier is to facilitate the research and private study of the student.

In Canada, the University of Alberta case (discussed above) held the making and circulation of extracts is legal under the 'private study, or research' exception. It also said 'instruction' and 'research' are fused purposes and should be read together and since students use these materials in the course of instruction and for private use, this is permissible fair dealing. In the United States of America, the *decision* in *Cambridge University Press* v. *Becker* clearly indicates that making of course packs without permission of the owners is permitted subject to a fair use threshold of 10%. This is also important because in the present Delhi University copyright dispute, a majority of reproduction is under 10%. There are similar legal precedents in several other countries as well.

4

(Un)Fair use in the Universities in India

You were born an original, don't die a copy!

— John Mason

[He was famous English Major General and Deputy Governor (1600-1672)]

4.0. Introduction

With the advent of Information and Communication Technology (ICT), the whole scenario of learning resources and its access and use pattern in the university libraries has drastically changed all over the world. Words like digital content, electronic library containing e-journals, e-books. journal consortiums, open access, digital library, DRM (Digital Rights Management) all have become simply buzzwords along with the traditional analog or print resources in the present library system. Our Indian Copyright Act, 1957 in its section 52 has listed various kinds of uses of copyrighted materials that are equally applicable for both analog as well as digital contents by which Copyright Act is not violated and these are the fair uses of the copyrighted materials. Considering the changing context and nature of content, use of copyrighted resources by the university academic communities in West Bengal, a highly educated and advanced state of India, is not different from the other developing nations of the world. Therefore it is appropriate to consider universities in developing nations as unique research objects thereby granting proper consideration to universities present in specific geographic locations. We must ensure that our prime objective of information dissemination is no way blocked by any law or act but at the same time we cannot afford to be cultural cops of the publishers. Thus we must formulate a sensible and balanced policy framework for our universities for better copyright management and access management to avoid all kinds of plagiarisms, litigation and above all for the promotion of scholarship and healthy academic culture. A research project sponsored by the UGC (completed in 2013) was carried out by the author as Principal Investigator to study fair use of copyrighted materials in the universities of West Bengal. The research finding of the study is quite disturbing. It is relevant and applicable in the universities of other states and developing nations with similar socio-economic structure.

4.1. Objectives of the study

1. To develop a fair use culture of the copyrighted materials among the principal stakeholders of the universities and above all in the higher academic institutions
2. Provide stimulus and encouragement to new creation
3. To make students, teachers, librarians and researchers aware in copyright and academic ethics to save themselves from unnecessary litigation.
4. Copyright mapping among the university libraries and its use pattern for fair use
5. To assess Access Management Policy and Copyright Management Policy (if any) for the universities

4.2. Research Questions

Present study seeks to assess how far fair uses of the copyrighted materials are being done in the universities. How the access of e-resources are managed in the universities. Answers were sought to the following research questions:

1. Are the copyrighted materials being used in the universities obeying the fair use principles?
2. Is there any copyright management policy in the universities?
3. Is there any access management policy for e-resources in the universities?

4.3. Assumption

"Copyrighted materials in the university libraries are being used according to the principles of fair use practices and there are well defined copyright management and access management policy in the universities."

4.4. Limitations

West Bengal is one of the most important states in India. Present study is limited to 12 Academic Universities, 3 Agricultural oriented Universities, 4 Topical Universities and 1 Open University in West Bengal (*table 1*). There are some new universities where libraries and its collection are still in developmental stage.

Table 1: Universities in West Bengal

Sl. No.	Name of the University	Analog /Print Collection	Digital Collection
Academic Universities			
1.	Jadavpur University	600,000 books & 1391 print journals	850 e-books, 9000 e-journals,15 databases
2.	University of Calcutta	Ten lakh books and more than 1500 print journals	e-books and e-journals & databases from almost all publishers, 4000 subscribed e-journals

3.	Rabindrabharati University	Approx. 1 lakh books and 304 print journals	e-resources accessed through UGC-Infonet programme
4.	University of Burdwan	1,58,962 books and 300 print journals	e-resources accessed through UGC-Infonet programme
5.	University of Kalyani	150000 books and 110 print journals	e-resources accessed through UGC-Infonet programme
6.	Vidyasagar University	71,877 books and 125 print journals	e-resources accessed through UGC-Infonet programme
7.	Viswa Bharati University	700000 books and print journals 20000	e-resources accessed through UGC-Infonet programme and 5000 e-books and 5000 e-journals, 2 databases
8.	University of North Bengal	1,59,552 books and 742 print journals	e-books and databases accessed through UGC-Infonet, 5550 e-journals
9.	University of Gour Banga	Library is in developmental stage	
10.	Aliah University	Library is in developmental stage	
11.	West Bengal State University	Library is in developmental stage	
12.	Indian Statistical Institute (ISI)	129000 books and 800 printed journals	700 e-books and 800 e-journals
Agricultural Universities			
1.	Uttar Banga krishi Viswabidyalaya	35000 books and 35 print journals	e-collections are being developed
2.	Bidhan Chandra krishi Viswabidyalaya	69460 books and 208 print journals	125 e-books, 175 e-journals and CeRA E-Resources Link (consortium for e-resources in Agriculture)
3.	West Bengal University of Animal and Fishery Sciences	17000 books and 80 print journals	CeRA E-Resources Link (consortium for e-resources in Agriculture)
Topical Universities			
1.	West Bengal University of Technology	Library is in developmental stage	
2.	The West Bengal	Library is in developmental stage	

	University of Health Sciences		
3.	Bengal Engineering and Science University	1.3 lakh books and many print journals	e-resources accessed through UGC-Infonet programme and INDEST
4.	National University of Juridical Sciences	14000 books	541 e- books and many law related e-journals
Open University			
1.	Netaji Subhas Open University	Approx. 10000 books	

4.5. Importance of the Study

Let us find out why and how the present study is relevant and important for the other parts of the world. Presently world population is 7 billion (approx.) and out of this, 6 billion (approx.) people live in developing or less developed countries (*PRB, 2011*). The world is becoming knowledge economy where acquiring knowledge through higher education has become important than ever before. It is quite understandable that number of universities and total enrolment in higher education in developing countries is far more than developed countries. They are chronically underfunded but face escalating demand - approximately half of today's higher education students live in the developing world (*Task Force on Higher Education and Society, World Bank 2000*). Characteristically universities in the developing nations including universities even in some European countries and in the Americas are of similar nature in terms of poor infrastructure, under qualified faculty, outdated teaching-learning process, underdeveloped curricula, poorly taught students, substandard research, non-transparent university governance and administration. Besides other parameters like low Gross Domestic Product (GDP) and low Purchasing Power Parity (PPP) contributes positively to the negative qualitative growth of the universities in the developing world. Low GDP and low PPP of a country clearly indicate poor affordability to purchase or access learning resources by the higher education students of that country. Almost all universities in the developing countries suffer from the same features. Products of the existing academic system in the developing countries specially from India and China serving everywhere in developed countries. Thus it would not be incorrect to focus on the universities in West Bengal, a state of India, as a developing nation represent the universities of other developing countries as a sample. This is how the present study is relevant also for universities in the other developing world.

University as a system promotes and propagates scholarship through the ages. It creates knowledge and also makes the premise for future research. Creation of new knowledge in every frontier is essential for human civilization. Traditionally Indian culture from the ages of the Vedas has always been emphasized on the purity of knowledge. Purity of knowledge stems from purity of contents on which future knowledge creation is dependent. Academic honesty and integrity are equally important during the creation of knowledge. It is a very delicate issue on which usually university academic community do not feel very comfortable. But issues are so important that is directly connected with country's economic development and potential impediment for becoming knowledge economy. Importance of the present study is that it has addressed the issue of fair dealing, academic integrity and copyright awareness among academic community in the universities of West Bengal as a representative sample of universities in the developing countries. It will surely help in identifying the points which must be redressed in order to bring well articulated and well defined copyright management policy in the universities of developing nations to promote and ensure quality of knowledge.

4.6. Literature Review

A primary mission of the University community is

the exchange and development of ideas and information. This brings us into daily contact with the expressions of those ideas embodied in print media, audio and video media, and computer media, among others. Universities are the producers as well as consumers of such expression. Many of the works containing these ideas are copyright protected and the consequences of infringement can be quite serious, therefore, an understanding of the impact of the copyright laws on our ability to utilize these works is very important.

Copyrights at universities are no longer incidental niceties of scholarship; they are increasingly the result of massive investments in equipment and personnel, and they are the deed of rights to potentially lucrative creations (Peterson, 1985). Courts originally developed fair use to dismiss cases of minute or socially beneficial infringements, and the doctrine was largely a rule of reason; courts could excuse and infringement if it "reasonably" should have been allowed (*Glenny and Dalglish, 1973*).

It is easy to imagine that a system seriously out of balance either way would hurt progress in science and the arts; no protection for authors might mean that fewer would be willing to invest the time and energy to create works; total control for authors or publishers over their works might severely restrict the public's use of the ideas contained in the works to develop new or derivative works or ideas. "Fair use" is the concept that provides balance between the two extremes (*Harper 1993*).

In the university context, however, fair use is intrinsically aligned with the notion that education deserves preferential treatment and should not be unduly inhibited. Fair use undoubtedly gives special deference to academic needs, although Congress and the courts have made clear that a non-profit educational purpose is no free license to appropriate protected works. Nor should it be. Any open-ended claim would eradicate scores of creative works that depend on copyright system for survival. Thus, fair use for education must be held to reasonable limits; within those limits a privilege for education is justified and indeed imperative for achieving copyright's goals (*Crews 1993*).

The world of copyright ownership in the university is in flux. This is a recent development. Before 1987, most believed that scholars owned their creative works, even though they were made for the classroom or during working hours. By owning one's creations under the "teacher exception," a teacher had freedom to use the works at other universities, make alternations and new creations from the initial works, and occasionally reap profit from publishing textbooks or, in rare cases, monographs. Today, the growing trend is to see the "teacher exception" as created not by judge-made law, but by individual university policies. Universities decide what they want to own and what they give *back* to the scholar/teacher creator (*Townsend 2003*).

4.7. Methods

The academic community of the universities as a population is subdivided into 3 subpopulations. The subpopulations are overlapping, and together they comprise the whole population. Subpopulations in the universities are in the following:

1. Librarians
2. Teachers
3. Researchers/students

The subpopulations are called *strata*. For collecting data, it is more appropriate if we consider *Stratified Random Sampling* (*Cochran, 2006*).

Reason for choosing this sampling technique is many but principal ones are:

a. Administrative conveniences like subpopulations are geographically distributed over a long distance.

b. Sampling problems with human population.

c. Heterogeneous population consists of subpopulations that are internally homogenous.

As the study is targeted to test the hypothesis and the study demands precise analysis of target concepts, questionnaire (both online as well as offline) was employed to collect the numerical data. Another reason for opting quantitative method for research is that it is more efficient than qualitative data.

From each subpopulation 100 individuals are randomly selected and approached to respond to the questionnaire. Of them Total 171 Stakeholders responded to the questionnaire through personal visit, sending online questionnaire (using Surveymonkey Web Platform) through e-mail, and uploading into the college library website (*http://librarybdc.webs.com/research.htm*). Of them 35 are Librarians including Deputy Librarians, Assistant Librarians (Grade I and II) and Information Scientists, 66 are University teachers including Professors, Associate Professors and Assistant Professors of Science, Arts, Commerce, Technology, Agricultural Science and Veterinary Science and 70 are Research Scholars/students in all the disciplines and University Students.

4.8. Result

There are 13 questions (*table 2*) in the questionnaire that were responded by the respondents.

Table 2. Questionnaire

Sl. No.	Questions	Yes	No
1.*	Are you aware of fair use of the copyright resources (analog as well as digital)?	53	118
2.*	Do you share your soft copies of research article(s)/ chapter(s) of a book or the whole book collected from your university e-library or digital library among your friends or others?	150	21

3.	The Government of India very recently introduced the Copyright (Amendment) Act, 2010 to comply with our International obligations and with the stated intention to making it fit for the purpose of digital age. Are you aware of it ?	20	151
4.*	Do you use Copyrighted works for only non-commercial purposes like teaching-learning/ research or not?	143	28
5.	Currently Fair Dealing only covers literary, dramatic, artistic, and musical works. Would you support the extension of fair dealing to cover computer programs, databases, sound recordings, film and broadcast?	98	73
6.	Do you support in the age of internet, you should be able to copy parts of a literary work, research article, parts of a news broadcast, film computer programs, databases and sound recordings?	162	09
7.*	Users should be able to copy the heart/core of a book or an article.	93	78
8.	Do you think there should be different laws for analog and digital resources and different laws should apply to their access?	133	38
9.	Users should be able to have a copy of a research article sent to his or her personal e-mail address rather than having to be present in the library or in the university.	155	16
10.*	Will you allow your books/research articles make publicly available in the web or using other means of broad dissemination?	41	130
11.*	Do you agree that to protect the interest of the copyright holder a library should monitor the material a user/researcher uses (even if the material is e-mailed, downloaded and accessed through his/her personal PC)?	42	129
12.*	Do you think sometimes it is needed to make multiple copies of book/articles other than for classroom teaching and distribute it to others?	109	62
13.*	Do you have a well-defined Access Management Policy and Copyright Management Policy in your university in order to stop all kinds of plagiarism and to retain academic integrity leading to academic excellence?	02	169

Here we consider 13 parameters for testing the hypothesis. But from the viewpoint of the hypothesis considering the few factors of fair use of copyrighted works, eight (marked with asterisk *) of them (assumed) are most responsible parameters. Factors of fair use are in the following:

- Factor 1 - Purpose of Use
- Factor 2 - Nature of Copyrighted Work
- Factor 3 - Relative Amount
- Factor 4 -Market Effect
- Factor 5- Intention

4.9. Analysis

We consider all parameters but mainly zeroed in on only those parameters/factors which are most suitable one for our purpose. For this we use one proportion test for each of the parameters.

Let p = Proportion of awareness of fair use of the copyright resources (analog as well as digital).

Null hypothesis, H_0: p e” 0.5 (it implies that people are aware of fair use of the copyright resources) against alternative hypothesis H_1: $p<0.5$. For this we use well-known statistical software (MINITAB version 13) and after computation we see that Sample proportion = 0.309942 and p-value<.0.05. Hence we conclude that awareness of fair use of the copyright resources (analog as well as digital) is not so popular among the academic community of the university. Similar deductions (*table 3 and 4*) are applicable to the rest of the parameters.

Table 3. Parameter-wise Null Hypotheses

Parameter	Null Hypothesis
1.*	Let p= Proportion of awareness of fair use of the copyright Null hypothesis, H_0: pe”0.5 against alternative hypothesis H_1: $p<0.5$.
2. *	Let p= Proportion of sharing of soft copies Null hypothesis, H_0: pe”0.5 against alternative hypothesis H_1: $p<0.5$.

3. Let p=Proportion of Awareness regarding Copyright Act/ Amendment

   Null hypothesis, H_0: pe”0.5 against alternative hypothesis H_1: $p<0.5$.

4. * Let p=proportion of use of copyrighted works for non-commercial purposes

   Null hypothesis, H_0: pe”0.5 against alternative hypothesis H_1: $p<0.5$.

5. Let p=proportion of preference of extension of fair dealing to e-resources

   Null hypothesis, H_0: pe”0.5 against alternative hypothesis H_1: $p<0.5$.

6. Let p=proportion of support for partial copying for e-resources

   Null hypothesis, H_0: pe”0.5 against alternative hypothesis H_1: $p<0.5$.

7.* Let p=proportion of preference to copy core of a book/article

   Null hypothesis, H_0: pe”0.5 against alternative hypothesis H_1: $p<0.5$.

8. Let p=proportion of liking for different laws for digital or e-resources

   Null hypothesis, H_0: pe”0.5 against alternative hypothesis H_1: $p<0.5$.

9. Let p=proportion of users like to have a soft copy of e-resources

   Null hypothesis, H_0: pe”0.5 against alternative hypothesis H_1: $p<0.5$.

10.* Let p=proportion of users likely to make their intellectual works available in the web/other means of free dissemination

   Null hypothesis, H_0: pe”0.5 against alternative hypothesis H_1: $p<0.5$.

11.* Let p= proportion of users likely to monitor their activities for e-resources access/uses

   Null hypothesis, H_0: pe”0.5 against alternative hypothesis H_1: $p<0.5$.

12.* Let p= proportion of users think making multiple copies is sometimes needed and its distribution

   Null hypothesis, H_0: pe”0.5 against alternative hypothesis H_1: $p<0.5$.

13.* Let p=Proportion of universities have access management policy and copyright management policy

   Null hypothesis, H_0: pe”0.5 against alternative hypothesis H_1: $p<0.5$.

Table 4. Parameter-wise p-value and inferences

Parameter	Sample Proportion	p-value	Inference
1. *	0.309942	p-value<.0.05	Users are not aware of fair use of the copyrighted works
2. *	0.877193	p-value>.0.05	Users like to share their e-resources
3.	0.116959	p-value<.0.05	Users are not aware of any Act/ Amendment
4.*	0.836257	p-value>.0.05	Copyrighted works are used for non-commercial purposes
5.	0.573099	p-value>.0.05	Users favour fair use of e-resources
6.	0.947368	p-value>.0.05	Users support partial copying of e-resources.
7. *	0.543860	p-value>.0.05	Users like to copy core of a book or an article
8.	0.777778	p-value>.0.05	Users want different laws for e-resources and its access
9.	0.906433	p-value>.0.05	Users like to own a copy of e-resources
10.*	0.239766	p-value<.0.05	Users disallow/dislike to make their intellectual works publicly available in the web or other means of free dissemination
11.*	0.245614	p-value<.0.05	Users do not like their access and use monitoring by the library
12.*	0.637427	p-value>.0.05	Users want to make multiple copies sometimes
13.*	0.011696	p-value<.0.05	Presently no University has any Access Management Policy and Copyright Management Policy

4.10. Discussion

From the above analysis of the resulted data, it is revealed that users of all categories are more or less equal in terms of copyright illiteracy. Very few of them are aware of fair uses of the copyrighted works and Copyright Act and subsequent Amendments. Though they have claimed that they use the resources for only non-commercial purposes but at the same time they likely to make multiple copies and its free distribution if the situation demands so. These two events are contrasting and their intentions are questionable. Users favour different laws for use and access of e-resources but in other hand they like to have own a soft copy of the e-resources for distribution and future uses. Users like to copy the core/heart of a book or an article but they do not want to share their intellectual works with others free of cost. Users do not want their activities (access/use of e-resources) are monitored by the library or by the appropriate authority. No university in the present study has either any well-defined Copyright Management Policy or any Access Management Policy for the encouragement of intellectual works, to restore high level of academic integrity and to combat plagiarism among academic community of the universities. Questions were intended for cross checking and designed to get corroborating evidences from the responses. It has showed very disturbing trend and not conducive for the promotion of scholarship, academic honesty and integrity and highly discouraging for the creators and innovators.

4.11. Findings

In the conclusion based on present analysis, it can be said that our primary hypothesis is completely rejected on the basis of above test and study. Thus we can say that copyrighted resources (both analog and digital) are being used in the universities in West Bengal without maintaining the principles of fair use practices. Presently there is no Access Management Policy and Copyright Management Policy in any University under the study. Thus it is highly recommended that academic community in the universities are made aware and literate about the copyright acts, specially to comply with the principles of fair use practices for the promotion of academic integrity, scholarship and to reward the creators and innovators.

Users must be educated and make them understand that with the inception of ICT and the revolution of internet and communication technology the conception of purchase of print (analog) resources are being replaced by the access and thus there must be Well-defined Access Management Policy in the Universities based on the principles of fair use practices.

To make a balanced copyright management and access management policy in the universities few other socio-economic factors of that nation must be considered otherwise the present situation will not improve. Universities should be well funded to promote copyright culture as poor affordability in the developing parts of world is one of the main factors of non-compliance of copyright. Degree of copyright compliance should be based on the economic conditions of the concerned country. It cannot be equated with the developed countries. International copyright laws, acts, treaties must be amended accordingly and should give equal opportunity of learning through equal access to the quality content among the higher education students of the developing nations. Universities may explore several paths to generate and collect fund to feed its research and other intellectual works.

Finally like in West Bengal, universities in the other developing nations need to design a well-defined Copyright Management Policy as well as a judicious funding policy, considering the holistic approach to improve the present situation, to combat the rampant plagiarism and to promote healthy copyright culture among the academic community.

5

Designing a Copyright Management Policy for Universities

Copyright law has got to give up its obsession with 'the copy.' The law should not regulate 'copies' or 'modern reproductions' on their own. It should instead regulate uses- like public distributions of copies of copyrighted work— that connect directly to the economic incentive copyright law was intended to foster. — **Lawrence Lessig**

(He is the Roy L. Furman Professor of Law at Harvard Law School & founder of Creative Commons)

5.0. Introduction

Neither ideas nor facts may be copyrighted. Copyright law protects the tangible expression of original works of authorship and describes the categories of works that may be copyrighted. Copyright owners have certain exclusive rights subject to some exceptions, including "fair use," which permits some limited use of copyrighted materials.

Copyright and universities; after years of discussion still a hot item. How can faculty achieve maximum access to scholarly information? How can universities raise awareness and educate their academics? How to process 'rights management' between the main stakeholders: authors, publishers and universities? (*Hofman, Linda-*

SURF, Collaborative organization for ICT in Dutch education and research in the Netherlands)

University copyright policies may be integrally related to the university's academic mission, but they are obviously rooted in the law. Without the system of legal rights and responsibilities, the policies would not exist.

Members of the University community routinely face issues under copyright law. Most issues relate to copyright ownership in new creative works or fair use of existing protected works. In addition, the University community manages existing copyrights, negotiates publication agreements, develops digital libraries, and reviews copyrighted materials before posting them on university websites or servers. Ability to access , its consumption and distribution to create some new works based on the pre-existing scholarly copyrighted works by the university community particularly faculty members, researchers and students have profound impacts on the advancement of learning and the promotion of scholarship. Effective copyright management can ensure the availability of scholarly content to the university community at reasonable terms. The purpose of this policy, beyond regulatory compliance, is to provide an overview of the fundamental principles of copyright law so as to assist the University community in addressing copyright issues.

5.1. International Guiding Principles

Now that IPR is considered as valuable assets, ownership in the hands of academics is not necessarily acceptable any longer to university authorities. Sometimes universities are seen to unable to secure copyright without proper contractual agreement in employment. However, finally every university is free to determine and choose its own suitable and sustainable path to resolve this contentious issue. In this context, before working out the basic copyright management plan for universities brief idea regarding the '*Tempe Principles*' and '*Zwolle Principles*' would make a sense and worth mentioning to grasp over the issue.

The 'Tempe Principles' that were adopted in Tempe, Arizona, on March 2-4, 2000, at a conference sponsored by the Association of American Universities, the Association of Research Libraries, and the Merrill Advanced Studies Center of the University of Kansas. The 'Tempe Principles' are in the following:

1. *The cost to the academy of published research should be contained so that access to relevant research publications for faculty and students can be maintained and even expanded. Members of the university community should collaborate to develop strategies that further this end. Faculty participation is essential to the success of this process.*
2. *Electronic capabilities should be used, among other things, to provide wide access to scholarship, encourage interdisciplinary research, and enhance interoperability and searchability. Development of common standards will be particularly important in the electronic environment.*
3. *Scholarly publications must be archived in a secure manner so as to remain permanently available and, in the case of electronic works, a permanent identifier for citation and linking should be provided.*
4. *The system of scholarly publication must continue to include processes for evaluating the quality of scholarly work and every publication should provide the reader with information about evaluation the work has undergone.*
5. *The academic community embraces the concepts of copyright and fair use and seeks a balance in the interest of owners and users in the digital environment. Universities, colleges, and especially their faculties should manage copyright and its*

limitations and exceptions in a manner that assures the faculty access to and use of their own published works in their research and teaching.

6. *In negotiating publishing agreements, faculty should assign the rights to their work in a manner that promotes the ready use of their work and choose journals that support the goal of making scholarly publications available at reasonable cost.*
7. *The time from submission to publication should be reduced in a manner consistent with the requirements for quality control.*
8. *To assure quality and reduce proliferation of publications, the evaluation of faculty should place greater emphasis on quality of publications and a reduced emphasis on quantity.*
9. *In electronic as well as print environments, scholars and students should be assured privacy with regard to their use of materials.*

The Joint Information System Committee (JISC), UK and SURF, the higher education and research partnership organization for network services and information and communications technology based in the Netherlands, initiated an international copyright project. The initiative became known as the "Zwolle Group," and it has significant contribution of developing and sharing guidance for the university community and other stakeholders to improve their management of copyright issues. SURF Foundation organized a working conference on 'Copyright and Universities' in December 2002 in Zwolle, the Netherlands. This endeavor produced landmark 'Zwolle Principles' which is not only unique in the world but also working as a guiding principles to design and develop an effective copyright management policy in universities.

The Zwolle Group Objective

To assist stakeholders – including authors, publishers, librarians, universities and the public – to achieve maximum access to scholarship without compromising quality or academic freedom and without denying aspects of costs and rewards involved.

The Zwolle Principles

1. *Achievement of this objective requires the optimal management of copyright in scholarly works to secure clear allocation of rights that balance the interests of all stakeholders.*
2. *Optimal management may be achieved through thoughtful development and implementation of policies, contracts, and other tools, as well as processes and educational programs, (collectively "Copyright Management") that articulate the allocation of rights and responsibilities with respect to scholarly works.*
3. *Appropriate Copyright Management and the interests of various stakeholders will vary according to numerous factors, including the nature of the work; for example, computer programs, journal articles, databases and multimedia instructional works may require different treatment.*
4. *In the development of Copyright Management, the primary focus should be on the allocation to various stakeholders of specific rights.*
5. *Copyright Management should strive to respect the interests of all stakeholders involved in the use and management of scholarly works; those interests may at times diverge, but will in many cases coincide.*
6. *All stakeholders in the management of the copyright in scholarly works have an interest in attaining the highest standards of quality, maximising current and future access, and ensuring preservation;*

stakeholders should work together on an international basis to best achieve these common goals and to develop a mutually supportive community of interest.

7. *All stakeholders should actively promote an understanding of the important implications of copyright management of scholarly work and encourage engagement with the development and implementation of Copyright Management tools to achieve the overarching objective.*

5.2. A Model Copyright Management Policy for Universities in India

Every university should have a written policy for copyright compliance. If your university doesn't have one, then persuade the seniors in the university administration and try to explain them its importance in higher education and advancement of scholarship so that an effective copyright policy can be devised in your university too. It might be possible that already different similar guidelines available in the university but they are not consistent to each other to have an integrated form. These fragmented guidelines should be joined based on the Indian Copyright Act, 1957 to have a united university copyright policy reflecting university's academic mission in a holistic view. Drafting any copyright policy is not enough until it is well-known as well as binding to the university community. Copyright researcher Paul Pedley outlines 3 key stages of developing a successful copyright policy but I suggest one more for its dynamisms and much effectiveness in a long run. In formulating a policy has two aspects-one is to protect your intellectual property and the other is to respect intellectual property rights of others.

Create a Policy
↓
Communicate the Policy & Make University Community Aware
↓
Enforce the Policy
↓
Feedback and Amendment for More Suitability & Embracing the Change

5.2.1. Basic principles

i. The university respects and intends to comply the provisions of the Indian Copyright Act, 1957 and its subsequent amendment from time to time in letter and spirit.

ii. The university respects the rights of copyright holders, their legitimate assertions of their rights and any rules that they articulate for the use of their material.

iii. Faculty members and students, researchers and other stakeholders require access to instructional materials that exist in both electronic and more traditional, non-electronic formats, and material in electronic form is entitled to the same protection as material in more traditional, non-electronic forms.

iv. The university has individual and collective responsibility to act responsibly in providing the materials that students, researchers, faculty members and other stakeholders require.

5.2.2. Objectives

1. Preserve and protect academic values that foster the free and creative expression and free exchange of ideas and the traditional practices and privileges with respect to the dissemination of scholarly works
2. Assure that the university's involvement in the creation of scholarly and instructional works is used to promote the broadest public good
3. Promote and support the use of information technology in the instructional, research, and

service missions of the university for the advancement of learning

4. Encourage members of the university community to be responsible users of copyrighted works and to take full advantage of fair use rights in their research, teaching, and service activities
5. to preserve traditional University practices and privileges with respect to the publication of scholarly works;
6. to establish principles and procedures for sharing income derived from copyrightable material produced at the University; and
7. to protect the University's assets and imprimatur
8. Minimise the risks associated with the improper use of copyright works
9. Demonstrate a commitment by the University and its highest level managers to a compliance culture.
10. Avoid unnecessary litigation that may arise out of unfair use of copyrighted materials

5.2.3. Rationale behind the University Copyright Management Policy

The rationale of this policy is to provide good administrative guidance on copyrightable works and ownership and to comply with the copyright laws. Besides, to define acceptable use of materials protected by copyright and to outline the responsibilities of all users of copyrighted materials in all media, and to establish a framework for fair and responsible practice.

5.3. Applicability of the Policy

This policy sets forth the rights and responsibilities of the university, its faculty, research scholars, students, and employees in their roles as members of the university community in creating and using copyrighted works. This policy is also applicable to all persons, including research collaborators, visiting researchers, consultants, and publishers whose copyrighted works result in whole or in part from the use of university facilities or resources.

5.4. Scope of the Policy

What it includes

1. This policy takes an overview of copyright laws and covers all printed, electronic and digital copyright material used within the scope of University activity. For the avoidance of doubt, this material includes, but is not limited to, text, images, databases, graphic designs, logos, sound recordings, films, broadcasts, computer programs (software) and electronic material stored on local and remote drives and on internet sites. Because the information technology environment is changing rapidly, it is impossible to envision every form of copyrightable work or the situation in which it might be created. As a result, this policy is broad, and is based on the principles described above.
2. This policy is solely concerned with issues relating to the use of third party material.

What it does not include

1. This policy does not cover the University's ownership of copyright in materials created by individual members of staff and students.
2. This policy does not cover use of University computers, data networks, e-mail or the Internet (internal or external web sites).

5.5. Responsibility of the members of the university

It is the responsibility of individual members of faculty members, staff, students or others stakeholders working on behalf of the University to make legitimate use of third party material. The exclusive rights of copyright holders should not be infringed. These exclusive rights are

- to copy the work
- to distribute copies to others
- to perform, show or play the work in public
- to communicate it to the public
- to make an adaptation or to do any of the above in relation to an adaptation.

Before copying or otherwise using material authored by others, the individual must determine whether that material is subject to copyright by considering whether the intended use is either

- lawful under statutory exception, "fair dealing" or other law, or
- permitted by license

If neither of the above applies, the individual must obtain permission from the copyright holder. This permission should be retained by the individual who requested it until such time as use of the copyrighted material is no longer required. If the copyrighted material is transferred to an archive, the permission documentation must be transferred also.

- ***Statement of Copyright Compliance and Copyright Clearance Form must be submitted***

  (Please see the Annexure I and Annexure II)
- ***Sample Letter Requesting Permission to Reproduce Copyrighted Material***

  (Please see the Annexure III)

Guidelines and Implementation

- The University provides detailed guidance on copyright law and the institutional licences to which it is a signatory on the Library web site
- Staff and students are expected to familiarize themselves with

such guidance and to apply it in all their dealings with copyright works.

- The University will place copyright notices adjacent to all relevant equipment that may be used for reproducing copyrighted materials. (Guidance specific to the acceptable use of University IT and photocopy facilities.)
- It is the responsibility of Deans and Heads of Department to ensure implementation of this Policy and its associated guidelines.
- Any misconduct or breach or violation relating to this policy by any users may lead to disciplinary action under the appropriate University procedures

General Responsibilities

- All members of the university community have the responsibility to respect the rights of copyright owners, to make themselves aware of the Indian Copyright Act and the exceptions outlined therein, and to take the steps necessary to ensure that their use of all copyright materials is compliant. The university has the responsibility to provide education and advice to all members of the university community on appropriate use, on the Copyright Act, and on exceptions.
- All members of the university community have the responsibility to recognize the important distinction between materials that are publically accessible via the Internet or other electronic means, and works that can be freely used.
- In addition to their personal responsibility for compliant use, faculty members also have a duty to inform their students of their responsibilities in their use of materials and advocate that students act with this responsibility in mind.
- Deans, department/unit heads and research account holders are responsible for taking reasonable steps to ensure effective implementation of this policy and to encourage continued compliance with it.
- The Copyright Coordinator and others who negotiate and handle licenses or contracts governing the use of copyright materials have the responsibility to make the terms of the agreements

available on request to interested parties and to assist with compliant use.

- The university has the responsibility to ensure the integrity of spaces where access is normally restricted, such as classrooms, both physical and virtual in nature, to ensure compliance with copyright agreements and legislation.

Non-compliance

- Non-compliance is a violation of federal legislation. In addition to any actions that might be taken by any copyright owner or licensing agent, the university will take action on any breaches of this policy.
- If there is reason to suspect that university policies have been, or are being violated, or that continued access to and use of copyright materials poses a threat to the reputation of the university, the university will take action.
- Following due process, the university may take action against anyone whose activities are in violation of this policy. The actions taken may include, but are not limited to:
- disciplinary action for employees
- disciplinary action for students under the appropriate regulations on academc dishonesty
- legal action that could result in criminal proceedings

Arbitration

- If a dispute arises between an Author or publisher any such right holders and the University with respect to the application of this Policy, the Author or publisher any such right holders and the University shall attempt to resolve the dispute through mediation, failing which the dispute shall be referred for decision to a panel composed of one member nominated by the Author or publisher any such right holders, one member nominated by the University and one member selected by the first two or, in the absence of an agreement between them, by the Dean of the Faculty of Law of the University.
- Until a decision is given by the panel, no action shall be brought by the Author or publisher any such right holders against the University or by the University against the Author or publisher

any such right holders, in any court of law on any matter arising out of this Policy.

5.6. Preamble

The University of .... (Name of the University) .... is dedicated to the creation, preservation, and dissemination of knowledge and ideas for the advancement of learning and promotion of scholarship through research, teaching, and service. The university is committed to creating knowledge and ideas for the improvement of the human condition, to preparing students to meet the needs of a changing society, and to advancing the wellbeing of our communities, state, nation, and world. The Indian Copyright Act, 1957 and its amendments from time to time provide the premise in establishing this copyright policy, University of .... seeks to create an environment in which its members will realize this worthy purpose.

5.7. Policy Principles

(a) The use of material created by others is central to the functions of the University as a public teaching, learning and research institution. The University supports and encourages the legitimate use of copyrighted materials to enhance the teaching, learning and research activities of the University.

(b) The University does not condone any use of copyrighted materials in breach of copyright laws, and expects all staff, students and other University community members to comply with copyright laws and all legal restrictions and obligations regarding the use of copyrighted material.

(c) Breaches of copyright law by members of the University community will be treated seriously as the risks that could flow to the University as a result of non-compliance with copyright are severe.

(d) The use of digital and online media in teaching is

encouraged and supported, as it enhances and streamlines the University's teaching functions. However, the University provides central coordination and management of the digitization and posting of copyrighted material through the Digital Resources Management Centre, so that the more complicated challenges and risks presented by online and digital media in terms of copyright compliance can be better managed.

5.8. Definitions

Classroom

This is any physical or virtual environment where access is normally restricted to class members or those granted access by the instructor. Certain exceptions to copyright legislation apply in the classroom.

Faculty Members

All those individuals responsible for teaching and instruction as per the concerned University statute or similar charter. Hereafter sametimes may be called as 'faculty' only.

Librarians

All those individuals receiving a letter of appointment from the appropriate authority of the university or that individuals to a professional librarian position, with or without compensation from the university, and whether full-time, research, part-time, visiting, or other status.

Project Staff

Persons working in any research project under any faculty member of the university those who have not directly registered for any research degrees under this university or any research institution with which this university has Memorandum of Understanding (MOU) for academic collaboration will be considered as project or research project staff.

Staff

All those individuals, in graded or ungraded positions, or on wage account status, whether full-time, part-time, or other status, receiving compensation from the university as employees, other than Faculty and Librarians.

Students

All individuals associated with the university in active student status as defined by formal registration, or on approved leave of absence status, whether full-time or part-time, whether or not holding a fellowship, a teaching assistantship, a research assistantship, or equivalent award, and whether or not receiving salary, wages, or a stipend.

Research Scholars

Any person who has attached to any department/ Centre/School of the concerned university under any supervisor working towards their higher research degrees like M.Phil or Ph.D or D.Litt or D.Sc. may or may not enjoying any fellowship for pursuing such degree will be considered as Research Scholars.

Sponsored Research

Refers to research activities or other work performed by Faculty, Librarians, Staff or Students under sponsorship from any agency

Sponsored

Party or parties external to the university, pursuant to an agreement between such agency or party and the university, which research activity or other work may result in the creation of copyrightable works.

Substantial Use

That use of university laboratory, studio, audio, audiovisual, video, television, broadcast, computer, computational or other facilities, resources and Staff or Students which: (i) falls outside the scope of the Faculty member's or Librarian's normal job responsibilities or the Student's academic program or (ii) entails a Faculty member's or Librarian's use of such resources that are not ordinarily available to all or virtually all Faculty members with comparable status in the same School or Department or to all or virtually all similarly situated Librarians.

Work Made for Hire

A work prepared by a Staff member or Student employed at the university within the scope of employment; or a specially commissioned work created by a Faculty member or Librarian within the scope of employment, as set forth in a specific written agreement between the Faculty member or Librarian and the university.

Transactional License

It is expressed permission for a specific use that has been secured from the copyright holder. Please keep a record of your permissions. *Please be aware that without permission, you will not be able to post or distribute the material.*

Fair Dealing

This is an exception to the *Copyright Act*, which permits the use of less than substantial passages and quotations from material protected by copyright for the purpose of private study, research, criticism, education, parody, satire, review and/or newspaper reporting (as per the Indian Copyright Act 1957; Section 52).

Public Domain

Works are those for which the term of copyright has expired. Generally, works enter the public domain in India 60 years following the end of the year in which the work's creator died.

Open Access

Is a movement in the distribution of scholarly material that requires works to be shared freely. "Free" means free of most copyright and licensing restrictions, yet are fully compatible with peer-review, copyright, profit and preservation

Creative Commons

Copyright licenses and tools offer a balance inside the traditional "all rights reserved" setting that copyright law creates. It gives creators a simple, standardized way to grant copyright permissions to their creative work and provides users with clear, understandable instructions on how materials can be used.

"Substantial Use" of university resources is that use of university laboratory, studio, audio, audiovisual, video, television, broadcast, computer, computational or other facilities, resources and Staff or Students which: (i) falls outside the scope of the Faculty member's or Librarian's normal job responsibilities or the Student's academic program or (ii) entails a Faculty member's or Librarian's use of such resources that are not ordinarily available to all or virtually all Faculty members with comparable status in the same School or Department or to all or virtually all similarly situated Librarians. The term "Substantial Use" does not include the use of personal office space, local telephone, library resources and personal computer equipment.

University premises include any location, physical or virtual, where (and when) the University instruction is delivered. University policies and practices govern behavior on University premises.

5.9. Category of Works and Rights

5.9.1. Category I: individual works, the copyright of which will normally belong to the faculty, librarians, staff or students or research scholars of the university

Scholarly Works

(a) The university makes no claim of ownership of copyright in works of authorship created by members of the university community, unless such works qualify as "Works Made for Hire" clause under Section 17 of the Indian Copyright Act determines who may be regarded as the 'first owner' of a copyrighted work or involve "Substantial Use" of university resources as defined above, or unless such works are created within the scope of a Sponsored Project under an agreement which provides for ownership of copyright by the university or a third party, in which case the Sponsored Project agreement shall take precedence. Sponsored Research, without a specific agreement in contrary to that, shall be considered scholarly work and the copyright in such works shall belong to the author(s), not to the university.

(b) The university strongly encourages Faculty members and Librarians who assign their copyright in scholarly publications to outside publishers to retain the royalty-free rights of reproduction and instructional use for themselves and for the university. Upon request, university administrators and legal expert will provide assistance relating to assignment agreements and such retention-of-rights clauses.

Textbooks and Instructional Materials

The university makes no claim of ownership of copyright in textbooks or other published instructional materials, including computer assisted and multimedia materials, unless said materials have been made with Substantial Use of university resources or qualify as Works Made for Hire as defined above.

Theses and Dissertations

Copyright ownership in a thesis or dissertation prepared by a Student toward degree requirements shall remain with the Student as primary author and Supervisors as secondary and subsequent authors based on their degree of supervisions, provided that, unless otherwise agreed in writing, by submitting the work for credit or degree requirements, the Student shall automatically be deemed to have granted a non-exclusive, worldwide, royalty-free license to the university (i) to make available for viewing to the university community through electronic or other means the entire thesis or dissertation; (ii) to make available to the broader public a limited number of copies of such thesis or dissertation, for which the university will make reasonable efforts not to reproduce and distribute in excess of ten copies per year of each such thesis or dissertation; and, (iii) to make a summary or abstract avaiiable to the university community and the public by electronic means without limitation on quantity of access or copying.

Faculty members and Librarians may make Substantial Use of university resources in creating copyrightable works within the scope of their job duties, with any usual or necessary approvals relating to the resource usage. Staff and Students, and Faculty and Librarians intending to work outside the scope of their university duties, shall not make Substantial Use of university resources to create copyrightable works without advance permission from, and an appropriate written agreement signed by, the relevant Vice President or designee. Failure to obtain such approval shall cause any copyrightable work created to be treated as Works Made with "Substantial Use" of University Resources.

Ownership of copyright in materials created by Faculty, Librarians, Staff or Students with "Substantial Use" of university resources shall be transferred by the author(s) to the, unless the university agrees, in writing, to waive or alter its rights. Notwithstanding the foregoing sentence, a transfer of copyright ownership by a faculty author to the university shall not be required if a work has been created with "Substantial Use" of university resources in accordance with the request or direction of the university, unless the faculty author and the university have entered into a specific written agreement governing copyright ownership with respect to the work.

5.9.2. Category II: Shared Rights

Prior Approval

Faculty members and Librarians may make Substantial Use of university resources in creating copyrightable works within the scope of their job duties, with any usual or necessary approvals relating to the resource usage. Staff and Students or Scholars, and Faculty and Librarians intending to work outside the scope of their university duties, shall not make Substantial Use of university resources to create copyrightable works without advance permission from, and an appropriate written agreement signed by, the appropriate authority. Failure to obtain such approval shall cause any copyrightable work created to be treated pursuant to breach of contract.

Transfer of Rights to University

Where a work subject to copyright is created with Substantial Use of university resources as provided above, unless otherwise agreed in writing, each Faculty member, Librarian, Staff, Researchers and Student author of such work shall execute an irrevocable written transfer, assignment or license to the university, in a form approved by the university, which provides for the following, unless otherwise disclosed by the Faculty member, Librarian, Staff or Student and, where relevant, agreed to by the university: a) That the author transfers all right, title and interest in and to the copyright to the university; b) that the work is an original work created by the author, that there are no known joint authors (or that any joint authors are or have been identified in writing to the university), and that the rights in such work have not been transferred, licensed or assigned to any other entity; c) that any pre-existing materials, whether copyrighted or in the public domain, reflected in the subject work, are or have been identified in writing to the university; d) that the author shall not distribute any copies of the work without the university's permission and that any copies of the work distributed by or with the authority of the author shall bear an appropriate copyright notice, and notice of the university's interest therein; and e) that the author shall execute any further documents, and provide any

5.9.3. Category III

Works Made with "Substantial Use" of University Resources.

Ownership of copyright in materials created by Faculty members, Librarians, Staff or Students or Research Scholars with "Substantial Use" of university resources shall be transferred by the author(s) to the university in accordance with policy for prior approval, unless the university agrees, in writing, to waive or alter its rights. Notwithstanding the foregoing sentence, a transfer of copyright ownership by a faculty author to the university shall not be required under this Section if a work has been created with "Substantial Use" of university resources in accordance with the request or direction of the university, unless the faculty author and the university have entered into a specific written agreement governing copyright ownership with respect to the work.

5.10. Copyright Administration

5.10.1. Disclosure of Category II and Category III Copyrightable Materials

Whenever any Student or Research Scholars or Staff member intends to create a copyrightable work that is outside the scope of the academic program or employment of a Student or Staff member and that may involve Substantial Use of university resources, that person shall disclose such intent to the Copyright Office of the university, in the form and manner approved by the university, to obtain in advance a tentative decision of the relevant official on whether the work will be a Work Made for Hire or will involve Substantial Use of university resources.

In addition, if at any time a Student or Research Scholars, Staff member, Faculty member or Librarian creates a copyrightable work that is a Work Made for Hire or involves Substantial Use of university resources, and such work or use of university resources has not received advance approval from the appropriate official, or if the basis on which an advance approval was given has materially changed, the Student or Research Scholars, Staff member, Faculty member or Librarian shall make a disclosure to and seek a decision from the appropriate official on whether creation of the work was Work Made for Hire or involved Substantial Use of university resources. Failure to comply with this Section may result in the forfeiture of the individual's rights

5.10.2. Registration, Deposit, Disposition and Protection of Copyright

Registration, deposit, disposition and protection of all copyrights owned by the university or in which the university has rights hereunder shall be accomplished in accordance with the university's directions, unless the university elects in writing to waive such rights with respect to any work and to transfer such rights to the author.

5.10.3. Copyright Administrator or Copyright Officer

A Collegium consists of all Head of the Departments (HODs) headed by anyone in the rank of Dean of any faculty (selected for the purpose) or any other dignitary with comparable status shall be the Copyright Administrator or Copyright Officer for the university. The Copyright Administrator shall ensure that the university's Copyright Policy is enforced and will supervise the preparation of copyright registrations and deposits for Category II and Category III copyrightable works, maintain records, and provide advice to Faculty, Librarians, Staff and Students or Research Scholars on copyrights and application of this policy.

5.10.4. Advisory Council

The Advisory Council on Research (which will include faculty representatives designated by the Faculty) will serve to assist the Copyright Administrator in the negotiation of copyright matters, the evaluation of ownership and the disposition of royalty income, primarily through its subcommittee.

5.10.5. Periodic Review

The university administration and the Faculty shall review this policy at least once every two years and, following such review, shall jointly determine whether modifications to the policy are necessary or desirable to best serve the interests of the university and its Faculty and Librarians, Staff, and Students or Research Scholars. Proposed amendments that result from such review and joint determination shall be presented to the University Council or Syndicate or the highest decision making authority of the university as applicable for final approval.

5.11. Commercialization

It is the mission of the university as a public institution to further education and research. University's resources are to be used solely for university purposes and not for personal nor for any other non-university purposes. Any commercialization of intellectual property should be consistent with these overriding purposes.

Before commercializing any work to which it owns the copyright, the university shall consult with the principal creator. Where there are commercial opportunities for a copyrightable work in which the university may have an ownership interest, the creator shall promptly disclose the work to the university. In cases of commercialization where direct competition with the university might exist, the creator shall consult with his or her dean prior to commercializing a work to which he/she owns the copyright. When the creator owns the copyright, he/she is encouraged to provide the university with the first opportunity to commercialize a work.

If the creator/copyright owner commercializes a work, the creator/copyright owner shall endeavor to retain for the university a non-exclusive, non-transferable royalty-free right to use the work within the university for educational, research, and public service purposes.

In cases where the university commercializes a work, any revenue sharing with the faculty creator shall be determined by a negotiated written agreement.

5.12. Statement of Responsibilities

5.12.1. The University has a responsibility to take reasonable steps to

(i) provide information and guidelines to employees, students, controlled entities and individuals associated with the University addressing their copyright rights and responsibilities;

(ii) develop, implement and support systems and processes that facilitate copyright compliance;

(iii) ensure there are financial, structural and administrative procedures in place to meet its obligations under copyright legislation, and review and revise these as required;

(iv) monitor external developments in relation to copyright, especially copyright legislation, to revise and update University policies, practices and documentation to adequately reflect changes, and to raise awareness of any developments as appropriate;

(v) ensure the University's corporate publications and information services, policies and facilities meet the requirements of the Copyright Act and are reviewed and revised periodically and as required;

(vi) respond appropriately to any alleged breaches of the Copyright Act brought to the attention of authorised officers of the University or of which officers become aware.

5.12.2. Specific copyright obligations

Responsibility: All teaching staff and their support staff; Course coordinators

(a) Teaching staff or other persons involved in the production, reproduction or delivery of teaching materials must be familiar with and meet their obligations as detailed in the Copyright Guidelines, including the proper labeling of educational material.

(b) Course coordinators have a responsibility to ensure copyright compliance of all material supplied to students enrolled in their courses, and to ensure that content posted on MyUni for the courses for which they are responsible is properly managed and complies with this Policy.

(c) When copyrighted materials or digital copies of broadcasts are to be made available as a teaching resource online or in other digital formats, staff must arrange the digitising and posting of the material through the Library's Digital Resources Management Centre.

(d) All staff posting other material online (such as website content or other MyUni materials) are responsible for ensuring the copyright compliance of their uploaded content and/or links to external material.

Responsibility: All staff and students in specialised areas

Staff, students including research scholars or other persons (including volunteers or contractors) who are engaged in areas where copyright issues regularly arise, such as the library, museums, Information Technology Services, press, Student Support Services , Archives must ensure that the specific copyright requirements applicable to their area of activity are complied with.

Responsibility: All staff and students publishing scholarly works

Where staff or students including research scholars are involved in the creation or publication of scholarly works, they must ensure that any copyrighted material of third parties is used lawfully. This may include warranting to the publisher that no third party copyright is infringed through the work. Where material is created or published in which the University is a joint copyright owner with one or more other parties, the staff or students involved in the project must ensure that the joint rights of the other parties are respected and must not recreate or republish that work without permission.

Commercial activities and self-financing courses
Responsibility: All staff

Where copyrighted material is to be used in connection with a commercial activity of the University, or in fee-for-service teaching, the use is not likely to be covered by the statutory licences authorising use for educational purposes. Staff or other persons involved in such activities on behalf of the University must ensure that appropriate arrangements are made to use the material in compliance with copyright laws. Advice must be sought from the Copyright Officer before material is used in such a manner.

Responsibility: Copyright Officer

(a) Provide professional advice to staff on the interpretation of the Act and this Policy upon request.

(b) Present education sessions through Centre for Learning and Professional Development, or upon request for Faculties or Schools.

(c) Maintain content on University Website for both staff and students.

(d) Advice to all university members to avoid any copyright conflict or potential dispute.

Faculty awareness

Responsibility : Deans (of different faculties)

(a) Raise awareness of this Policy within their Faculty.

(b) Encourage existing staff to undertake the copyright online induction or orientation course.

Staff education

Responsibility : Director, UGC-Human Resource Development Centre (HRDC) or any such centre for teaching-learning

(a) Ensure that dedicated training sessions on copyright

and responsibilities are made available to staff on a regular basis (and at least twice per academic year).

(b) Ensure that training on copyright issues is incorporated wherever possible into other academic staff training sessions, such as the orientation programme or refresher courses or short term courses or any workshop

Analog and Digital Resources

Responsibility : University Librarian

(a) Oversee the Digital Resources Management Centre's management of online material.

(b) Oversee the access management to ensure copyright compliance attuned with this copyright management policy

(c) Oversee the use of Library holdings and facilities generally, consistent with this Policy.

5.13. Copyright Clearance

5.13.1. Guidelines

1. Teachers, instructors, professors and staff members in non-profit universities may communicate and reproduce, in paper or electronic form, short excerpts from a copyright-protected work for the purposes of research, private study, criticism, review, news reporting, education, satire or parody.
2. Copying or communicating short excerpts from a copyright-protected work under this Fair Dealing Policy for the purpose of news reporting, criticism or review must mention the source and, if given in the source, the name of the author or creator of the work.
3. A copy of a short excerpt from a copyright-protected work may be provided or communicated to each student enrolled in a class or course:

(a) as a class handout

(b) as a posting to a learning or course management system that is password protected or otherwise restricted to students of the university

(c) as part of a course pack

4. A short excerpt means:

(a) up to 10% of a copyright-protected work (including a literary work, musical score, sound recording, and an audiovisual work). This 10 % does not qualify for qualitative copying but quantitative copying only and it should be strictly implemented.

(b) one chapter from a book

(c) a single article from a periodical

(d) an entire artistic work (including a painting, print, photograph, diagram, drawing, map, chart, and plan) from a copyright-protected work containing other artistic works

(e) an entire newspaper article or page

(f) an entire single poem or musical score from a copyright-protected work containing other poems or musical scores

(g) an entire entry from an encyclopedia, annotated bibliography, dictionary or similar reference work provided that in each case, no more of the work is copied than is required in order to achieve the allowable purpose.

5. Copying or communicating multiple short excerpts from the same copyright-protected work, with the intention of copying or communicating substantially the entire work, is prohibited.

6. Copying or communicating that exceeds the limits in this Fair Dealing Policy may be referred to the Copyright Officer for evaluation. An assessment of

whether the proposed copying or communication is permitted under fair dealing will be made based on all relevant circumstances.

7. Any fee charged by the university for communicating or copying a short excerpt from a copyright-protected work must be intended to cover only the costs of the university, including overhead costs.
8. Copying or communicating from licensed electronic resources is governed by the terms of the University's licenses with the vendors and publishers of those resources. If there is a conflict between the terms of such a license and the terms of the Fair Dealing policy, the terms of the licence of e-resources (ebooks, ejournals, and databases) will prevail.

5.13.2. Individuals have a responsibility to

(i) make a reasonable effort to become aware of their rights and obligations in relation to copyright, including moral rights obligations;

(ii) adhere to the requirements of the Indian Copyright Act,1957 apply University policies, practices and procedures when using copyright works;

(iii) consult with the Copyright Office when preparing unit materials supplied to, or made accessible to enrolled students, to ensure compliance with the relevant copyright law requirements, licence conditions, and University processes;

(iv) consult with the Copyright Office prior to entering into agreements with outside organisations on behalf of the University, particularly when third party copyright material has been used;

(v) report any alleged breaches of copyright of which they are aware to an appropriate Copyright Office.

5.14. Policy Implementation

i. The University provides detailed guidance on copyright law and the institutional licences including terms and conditions for access to the digital resources to which it is a signatory on the Library web site.

ii. Staff and students are expected to familiarise themselves with such guidance and to apply it in all their dealings with copyrighted works.

iii. The University will place copyright notices adjacent to all relevant equipment that may be used for reproducing copyrighted materials.

iv. If staff or students of the University are in any doubt about their proposed reproduction or use of third-party copyright works, they may contact the Copyright Officer for further advice and assistance.

v. It is the responsibility of Deans and Heads of Department to ensure implementation of this Policy and its associated guidelines.

vi. Any misconduct or breach relating to this policy by any University employee may lead to disciplinary action under the appropriate University procedures

vii. Policy violations by students including research scholars will be dealt with as cases of academic misconduct and standard disciplinary procedures will apply.

5.14.1. Dealing with alleged breaches of copyright

(a) Breaches of copyright law by members of the University community will be treated seriously by the University. Staff and students respectively may face disciplinary action if they fail to comply with this Policy and the legal requirements relating to copyright.

(b) Where a staff member, student including research

scholars or some other member of the University community believes that the availability of any material on the University's library system may be in breach of copyright, that potential infringement must be reported to the Copyright Officer in accordance with the Procedure for Take-Down Notices and Other Copyright Complaints made under this Policy.

(c) Where a notice is received from outside the University alleging that the availability of any material on the University's library system or any such system may be in breach of copyright, the notice must be forwarded to the Copyright Officer in accordance with the Procedure for Take-Down Notices and Other Copyright Complaints made under this Policy.

5.15. Authorities

The following authorities (Fig. 6.) are delegated under this Policy:

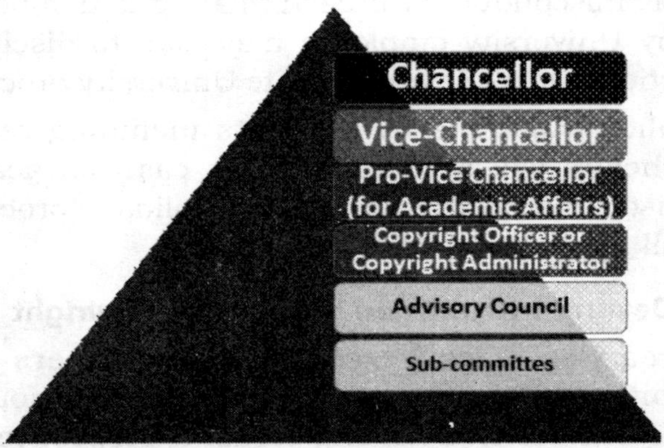

Fig. 6. Delegations of Authority

Any dispute or any conflict on copyright related issues in the university the right of final say will be bestowed on the Chancellor of the University. Any such case forwarded by the Copyright officer will be submitted to the Pro-Vice Chancellor (for Academic Affairs) for his advice. If still it is unresolved it may be submitted to the Vice-Chancellor of the university who may seek the advice and suggestions on the issues in question from the University Council or Syndicate. Based on their advice the existing copyright management policy may be suitably amended. Whatever may be the decision of the university council or syndicate headed by the Vice-Chancellor must be approved by the Chancellor finally to put it into action for execution or implementation as applicable.

6

Fair Use in SAARC Countries

"Much of the unprecedented economic growth of the past 10 years can actually be credited to the doctrine of fair use, as the Internet itself depends on the ability to use content in a limited and nonlicensed manner,"

— Computer and Communications Industry Association (CCIA), US

6.0. Introduction: Fair Use or Fair Dealing Provisions in SAARC Countries

The fair use doctrine encourages member of the citizenry to create and innovate and get inspired from the pre-existing works. A recent study in the US showed that the value added to the U.S. economy by copyright industries amounts to $1.3 trillion whereas the value added to the U.S. economy by the fair use amounts to $2.2 trillion. The fair use economy's "value added" is thus almost 70% larger than that of the copyright industries. It is an exemption towards creative use of the copyrighted materials. Fair use can be said as functional tool for promoting economic activity. Thus the fair use economy is greater than the copyright economy.

The SAARC (The South Asian Association for Regional Cooperation) was established in Dhaka in Bangladesh in 1985 comprising of 8 neighboring countries (*Afghanistan, Bangladesh, Bhutan, India, Maldives, Nepal, Pakistan, and Sri Lanka*) having more or less same socio-economic condition. Fair use or fair dealing provisions in respective copyright and related rights act of the SAARC countries have been juxtaposed in the following and this will help us sharing their thoughts on fair use for further research and extending its scope in our national laws.

6.1. Afghanistan

Since 2008 copyright in Afghanistan has been governed by the law on the support the right of authors, composers, artists and researchers (Copy Right Law). Its article 40 few provisions are there as an exception to the copyright.

Situations of Use of work and adoption

Article 40

1. It shall be lawful to reproduce short Works or extracts of Works for teaching purposes in educational institutions the activities of which do not serve direct or indirect commercial gain, provided that:

   The act of Reproduction is an isolated one occurring, if repeated, each occurring should be on separate and unrelated occasions.

   There is no collective license available for Reproduction by a competent authority in the collective management of rights of which the educational institution is or should be aware.

   The name of the Author and the title of the Work shall be indicated on all copies.

2. Copying and replication of a Work for the purpose of using it, is lawful under the following conditions:

   the user does not make direct or indirect commercial gains.

   Where the published article is a summary or an extract of the Work and Reproduction is to satisfy the personal needs, provided that: The library or archive makes sure that the copy will be used solely for the purposes of study, scholarship or research, and if repeated, each occurring should be on separate and unrelated occasions, and There is no collective license available for Reproduction by a competent authority in the collective management of rights of which the library or archive is or should be aware.

3. The Reproduction is permitted where the copy is made with the aim of preserving the original copy or, when necessary, replacing a lost, destroyed or rendered unusable copy in the permanent collection of another similar library or archive, provided that: It is impossible to obtain such a copy under reasonable conditions; The act of Reproduction or photocopy is an isolated one occurring case.

6.2. Bangladesh

The basic legal instrument governing copyright law in Bangladesh is the Copyright Act, 2000. It is largely based on Pakistan's Copyright Ordinance, 1962. Certain acts are said not to constitute an infringement of copyright (section 72).

1. The following acts shall not constitute an infringement of copyright, namely:
   (a) Fair use of a literary, dramatic, musical or artistic work for the purpose of—
      (i) private study or private use including research;
      (ii) criticism or review, whether of that work or of any other work;
   (b) Fair use of a literary, dramatic, musical or artistic work for the purpose of reporting current events—
      (i) in a newspaper, magazine or similar periodical, or

(ii) by broadcast or in a cinematographic work or by means of photograph....

6.3. Bhutan

The Copyright Act of the Kingdom of Bhutan, 2001 has following provisions as copyright exceptions.

Private Reproduction for Personal Purposes

10(1) Notwithstanding the provisions of Section 8(1) (a), and subject to the provision of subsection (2), the private reproduction of a published work in a single copy, where the reproduction is made by a physical person exclusively for his own personal purposes, shall be permitted, without the authorization of the author of, or other owner of the copyright in, the work. (2) The permission under subsection (1) shall not extend to the reproduction a. of a work of architecture in the form of building or other construction; b. where the reproduction is repro graphic reproduction, or ari entire book, or a substantial part thereof, or of a musical work in graphic form; c. of a data base; d. of a computer program, except as provided in Section 15; and e. of any work in cases where reproduction would conflict with a normal exploitation of the work or would otherwise unreasonably prejudice the legitimate interests of the author of, or other owner of the copyright in, the work.

Quotation

11. Notwithstanding the provisions of Section 8(1)(a), the reproduction of a short part of a published work, in the fonn of quotation, in another work, shall be pennitted without authorization of the author of, or other owner of the copyright in, the work from which the quotation is taken, provided that such a reproduction is compatible with fair practice and its extent does no ' t exceed the extent justified by the purpose. The quotation shall be accompanied by the indication of its source and the name

of the author if his name appears in the work from which the quotation is taken.

Reproduction for Teaching

12. (1) Notwithstanding the provisions of Section 8(1)(a), the following acts shall be permitted without the authorization of the author of, or other owner of the Copyright in, the work : a. the reproduction of a short part of a published work, by way of illustration, in writings or sound or visual recordings for teaching, provided that i) such reproduction is compatible with fair practice, and ii) its extent does not exceed the extent justified· by the purpose;

b. the reprographic reproduction, for face-to-face teaching in educational institutions whose activities do not serve direct or indirect commercial gain, to the extent justified by the purpose, of a published article or other short work or short extract of a writing, with or without illustrations, provided that i) the act of reproduction is an isolated one occurring, if repeated, on separate and unrelated occasions, and ii) there is no collective license available (that is, offered by a collective administration organization in a way that the educational institution is aware or should be aware of the availability of the license) under which such reproduction can be made. (2) On any copy made under paragraph (1), its source and the name of the author shall be indicated, as far as practicable.

Reprographic Reproduction by Libraries and Archives

13. Notwithstanding the provisions of Section 8(1) (a), a library or archive whose activities do not serve direct or indirect gain may, without the authorization of the author of, or other owner of copyright in, the work, make a single copy of the work by reprographic reproduction. a. where the work reproduced is a published article or other short work or short extract of a writing, with or without illustrations, and where the purpose of the

reproduction is to satisfy the request of a physical person, provided that i) the library or archive is satisfied that the copy will be used solely for the purpose Of study, scholarship or private research, ii) the act of reproduction is an isolated case occurring, if repeated, on separate and unrelated occasions, and iii) there is no collective license available (that is, offered by a collective administration organization in a way that the library or archive is aware or should be aware of the availability of the license) under which such copies can be made; or b. where the making of such a copy is in order to preserve and, if necessary (in the event that it is lost, destroyed or rendered unusable), replace a copy, or to replace, in the permanent collection of another similar library or archive, a copy which has been lost, destroyed or rendered unusable, provided that —

(i) it is impossible to obtain such a copy under reasonable conditions, and

(ii) the act of reprographic reproduction is an isolated case occurring, if repeated, on separate and unrelated occasions.

Reproduction, Broadcasting and Other Communication to the Public for Informatory Purposes

14. Notwithstanding the provisions of Section 8(1)(a), (h) and (i), the following acts shall be permitted, without the authorization of the author of, or other owner of copyright in, the work, subject to the obligation to indicate, as far as practicable, the source and the name of the author:

(a) the reproduction in a newspaper or periodical, the broadcasting or other communication to the public, of an article published in a newspaper or periodical on current economic, political or religious topics or a broadcast work of the same character; this permission shall not apply where the right to authorize reproduction, broadcasting or other communication to the public is expressly reserved by the author, or other owner of copyright, on the copies, or in connection with the broadcasting or other communication to the public, of the work;

(b) the reproduction and the broadcasting or other communication to the public, for the purpose of reporting current events, of short excerpts of work seen or heard in the course of such an event, to the extent justified by the said purpose;

(c) the reproduction in a newspaper or periodical, the broadcasting or other communication to the public of a political speech, a lecture, address, sermon or other work of similar nature delivered in public, or a speech delivered during legal proceedings, the extent justified by the purpose of providing current information.

Reproduction and Adaptation of Computer Programs

15. (1) Notwithstanding the provisions of Section 8(1)(a) and (c), the reproduction in one copy of the adaptation of a computer program shall be pennitted, without the authorization of the author of, or other owner of copyright in, a computer program, by the lawful owner of a copy of that computer program, provided that the copy or adaptation is necessary.

a. for the use of the computer program in conjunction with a computer for the purpose, and to the extent, for which the computer program has been obtained; for archival purposes, and, for the replacement of the lawfully owned copy of the computer program i,of the computer program is lost, destroyed or rendered unusable.

(2) No copy or adaptation mentioned in subsection (1) shall be used for any purpose other than the ones determined in subsection (1), and any such copy or adaptation shall be destroyed in the event that continued

possession of the copy of the computer program ceases to be lawful.

Importation for Personal Purposes

16. Notwithstanding the provisions of Section 8(1) (f), the importation of a copy of a work, by a physical person, for his personal purposes, shall be permitted without the authorization of the author of, or other owner of copyright in, the work.

6.4 India

(*Please refer to Chapter 1 Section 1.8*)

6.5 Maldives

The copyright and related rights act of Maldives was enacted n October 21, 2010.

Following sections has mentioned few uses that may be eligible to get copyright exemption as fair use.

Private Reproduction for Personal Purposes

12. (a) Notwithstanding the provisions of Section 10 (a) (1), and subject to the provisions of Subsection (b), the private reproduction of a published work in a single copy shall be permitted without theauthorization of the author or owner of copyright, where the reproduction is made by a person exclusively for his own personal purposes.

(b) The permission under Subsection (a) shall not extend to the following.

(1) to the reproduction of a work of architecture in the form of building or other construction;

(2) to reproduction in the form of the whole or a substantial part of a book or of a musical work in the form of notation;

(3) to reproduction of the whole or a substantial part of a database in digital form;

(4) to reproduction of a computer program, except as provided in Section 18 of this regulation; and

(5) to reproduction of any work in cases where reproduction would affect the normal proceedings the work may generate and could prejudice the legitimate interests of the author or other owner of the copyright.

(6) to reproduction of feature films, documentary films, dramas, video songs and other audiovisual presentations created for commercial use.

Temporary Reproduction

13. Notwithstanding the provisions of Section 10 (a)(1), the temporary reproduction of a work shall be permitted if all the following conditions are met;

(a) the reproduction is made in the process of a digital transmission of the work or while making a digitally stored work perceptible,

(b) the reproduction is by a person or entity with the authorization of the owner of copyright or is entitled to it by law.

(c) it is an accessory to that transmission or making perceptible, that occurs during the normal operation of the equipment used and results in the automatic deletion of the copy without enabling the retrieval of the work for any other purpose than those specified in items (a) and (b).

Quotation

14. (a) Notwithstanding the provisions of Section 10 (a) (1), the reproduction in the form of quotation, of a short part of a published work shall be permitted without authorization of the author or other owner of copyright, provided that the reproduction is compatible with fair practice and does not exceed the extent justified by the purpose.

(b) The quotation shall be accompanied by an indication of source, the name of the author, and form of publication as far as practicable of the provisions specified in (a) of this Section.

Reproduction for Teaching

15. (a) Notwithstanding the provisions of Section 10 (a) (1), a limited portion of a published work can be reproduced and presented as a quotation without the authorization of the author or other owner of copyright, provided that such reproduction is compatible with fair practice and does not exceed the extent justified by the purpose;

(b) The reproduction shall be accompanied by an indication of source, the name of the author, and form of publication as far as practicable of the provisions specified in (a) of this Section.

Reprographic Reproduction by Libraries and Archives

16. Notwithstanding the provisions of Section 10 (a) (1), any library or archive whose activities do not serve direct or indirect commercial gain may, without the authorization of the author or other owner of copyright, make a single copy of the work by reprographic reproduction in the following ways.

(a) where the work reproduced is a published article, other short work or short extract of a work, and where the purpose of the reproduction is to satisfy the request of a particular person, provided that;

(1) the library or archive is satisfied that the copy will be used solely for the purpose of study, scholarship or private research,

(2) the act of reproduction is an isolated case occurring, if repeated, on separate and unrelated occasions, and(3) there is no collective license available that is, offered by a collective administration organization of which

the library or archive is or should be aware, under which such copies can be made; or

(b) Where the copy is made in order to preserve and if necessary, replace a copy or to replace a copy which has been lost, destroyed or rendered unusable in the permanent collection of another similar library or archive, provided that it is impossible to obtain such a copy under reasonable conditions, and provided further that the act of reprographic reproduction is an isolated case occurring, if repeated, on separate and unrelated occasions.

Reproduction, Broadcasting and Other Communication to the Public for Informatory Purposes

17. Notwithstanding the provisions of Section 10 (a), (8) and (9), the following acts shall be permitted in respect of a work without the authorization of the author or the other owner of the copyright, subject to the obligation to indicate the source and the name of the author as far as practicable:

(a) the reproduction in a newspaper or periodical, the broadcasting or other communication to the public of an article published in a newspaper or periodical on current economic, political or religious topics or a broadcast work of the same character. This permission shall not apply where the right to authorize reproduction, broadcasting or other communication to the public is expressly reserved on the copies by the author or other owner of copyright, or in connection with broadcasting or other communication to the public of the work;

(b) the reproduction in a newspaper or periodical, the broadcasting or other communication to the public of a political speech, a lecture, sermon or other work of similar nature delivered in public, or a speech delivered during legal proceedings, to the extent justified by the purpose of providing current information; and

(c) for the purpose of reporting current events, the reproduction and the broadcasting or other communication to the public of short excerpts of a work seen or heard in the course of such events, to the extent justified by the purpose.

Reproduction and Adaptation of Computer Programs

18. (a) Notwithstanding Section 10 (a) (1) and (3), the reproduction, in a single copy, or the adaptation of a computer program by the lawful owner of a copy of that computer program shall be permitted without the authorization of the author or other owner of copyright, provided that the copy or adaptation is necessary for the following.

(1) for use of the computer program with a computer, for the purpose and extent for which the computer program has been obtained; or

(2) for archival purposes and for the replacement of the lawfully owned copy of the computer program in the event that the said copy of the computer program is lost, destroyed or rendered unusable.

(b) No copy or adaptation of a computer program shall be used for any purpose other than those specified in (a) of this Section. In the event that continued possession of the copy of the computer program ceases to be lawful, the relevant government authority has the power to destroy any such copy or adaptation without compensation.

Display of Works

19. Notwithstanding the provisions of Section 10 (6) of (a), the public display of originals or copies of works shall be permitted without the authorization of the author, provided that the display is made other than by means of a film, slide, television image or otherwise on screen or by means of any other devise or process, and provided

further that the work has been published or the original or the copy displayed has been sold, given away or otherwise transferred to another person by the author or his successor in title.

6.6. Nepal

The Copyright law of Nepal governs copyright, the right to control the use and distribution of artistic and creative works in Nepal and also encourages the creation of art and culture by rewarding authors and artists with a set of exclusive rights.[1] It is embodied in the Copyright Act, 2059 (2002), the Copyright Rule, 2061 (2004) and their amendments. Chapter 4 (Section 16-23) of the copyright law consists of few Circumstances where the copyrighted materials can be used without authorization

Chapter 4 : Circumstances where the copyrighted materials can be used without authorization

16. Reproduction allowed for personal purpose: (1) Notwithstanding anything contained in Clause (a) of Section 7, no authorization shall be required from the author or the copyright owner to reproduce some portions of any published work for personal use.

(2) Notwithstanding anything contained in Sub-section (1), no reproduction of an aıchitectural design erected as a building and other construction related design or a significant portion of any book or of a musical work as notation of all or significant portion of a database through digital transmission shall be allowed in a manner to be prejudicial to the economic right of the author or the copyright owner.

17. Citation allowed : Notwithstanding anything contained in Clause (a) of Section 7, some portions of a published work can be cited for fair use without authorization of the author or the copyright owner in a manner not to be prejudicial to the economic right of such author or owner. In making such citation, its source and the author' name, in cases where it appears, shall also be mentioned.

18. Reproduction allowed for teaching and learning : (1) Notwithstanding anything contained in Clause (a) of Section 7, the following acts may be done for teaching and learning activities without authorization of the author or the copyright owner in a manner not to be prejudicial to the economic right of such author or owner:

To reproduce a small portion of any published work by way of citation, writing or audio-visual aid,

To reproduce, broadcast and exhibit some portions of the work for purposes of educational activities to be performed in the classroom.

(2) All copies reproduced pursuant to Sub-section (1) have to indicate the source and the author's name.

19. Reproduction by library and archives : Notwithstanding anything contained in Clause (a) of Section 7, in cases where a public library or archives, which makes available the work stored in it at the request of a person doing research or study without deriving economic profits directly or indirectly, looses any work with it or such work is destroyed or is old or is incapable of being obtained, it may reproduce one copy of such a work without authorization of the author or the copyright owner of such work.

20. Reproduction, broadcast and other communication allowed for purposes of information to the general public : (1) Notwithstanding anything contained in clauses (a), (i) and (j) of Section 7, the following acts can be done, by mentioning the sources and name of the author of any work, without authorization of the author or the copyright owner of such work.

To print in any newspaper or journal or to make broadcast or other communication to public of any article,

article under political or religious topics or similar other broadcasts published in any newspaper or journal.

Provided, however, that such act shall not be prejudicial to the economic right of the author or the copyright owner.

To reproduce, broadcast or otherwise communicate or justify any event with a view to informing the general public about any current event.

To reproduce, broadcast or to make communication to public some portions of any regular newspaper or journal regularly publishing information for communication to the general public or pleadings made on court proceedings with a view to disseminating current information.

(2) Notwithstanding anything contained in Sub-section (1), in cases where the author himself/herself has indicated that his/her work is prohibited from being reproduced, broadcast and other kinds of communications, no reproduction, broadcasting and other communication shall be allowed.

21. Reproduction of computer program : Notwithstanding anything contained in Clauses (a) and (c) of Section 7, in cases where the objectives for which a computer program was acquired could not be achieved or with a view to maintaining records or where the computer program acquired legally is lost or destroyed or is incapable of being used, one copy of the computer program can be reproduced without authorization of its author or copyright owner.

22. Importation allowed for personal purposes : Notwithstanding anything contained in Clauses (g) of Section 7, one copy of any work can be imported for personal purpose, without authorization of its author or copyright owner.

23. Public exhibition allowed : Notwithstanding anything contained in clauses (h) of Section 7, in cases where any person intends to have public display of any work or copy of the work, he may do so without authorization of its author or copyright owner.

Provided, however, that such public display has to be made without the help of film, slide, television image or otherwise using the screen or device of other kind.

6.7. Pakistan

The basic legal instrument governing copyright law in Pakistan is the Copyright Ordinance, 1962 as amended by the Copyright (Amendment) Ordinance, 2000.

Certain acts are said not to constitute an infringement of copyright (s. 57). These include *inter alia*

- fair dealing with a literary, dramatic, musical or artistic work for the purpose of research, private study, criticism, review (cl. a) or reporting current events (cl. b)
- in relation to a literary or dramatic work in prose: single extract up to 400 words, or a series of extracts (with comments interposed) up to a total of 800 words with no one extract exceeding 300 words (expl. i)
- in relation to a literary or dramatic work in poetry: extract up to a total of 40 lines and in no case exceeding one fourth of the whole (expl. ii)
- the reproduction or adaptation of a literary, dramatic, musical or artistic work by a teacher or a pupil for the purpose of instruction or examination (cl. h)
- the performance of a literary, dramatic or musical work by the staff and students of an educational institution (cl. i)
- the making of up to 3 copies of a book by a public or non-profit library for its use if such book is not available for sale (cl. o)

- the reproduction or publication of certain Government works (unless prohibited; cl. q)
- the making or publishing of a painting, drawing, engraving or photograph of an architectural work of art (cl. r) or a sculpture or other artistic work if such work is permanently situated in a public place (cl. s)

6.8. Srilanka

The basic legal instrument governing copyright law in Sri Lanka is Part II (ss. 5–27) of the Intellectual Property Act, No. 36 of 2003 PART II – CHAPTER 1

Fair use

11. (1) Notwithstanding the provisions of subsection (1) of section 9, the fair use of a work, including such use by reproduction in copies or by any other means specified by that section, for purposes such as criticism, comment, news reporting, teaching (including multiple copies for classroom use), scholarship or research, shall not be an infringement of copyright.

(2) The following factors shall be considered in determining whether the use made of a work in any particular case is fair use:

(a) the purpose and character of the use, including whether such use is of a commercial nature or is for non-profit educational purposes;

(b) the nature of the copyrighted work;

(c) the amount and substantiality of the portion used in relation to the copyrighted work as a whole; and

(d) the effect of the use upon the potential market for, or value of, the copyrighted work.

(3) The acts of fair use shall include the circumstances specified in section 12.

Acts of fair use

12. (1) Notwithstanding anything contained in paragraph (a) of subsection (1) of section 9 and subject to the provisions of subsection (2) of this section, the private reproduction of a published work in a single copy shall be permitted without the authorization of the owner of the copyright, where the reproduction is made by a physical person from a lawful copy of such work exclusively for his own personal purposes.

(2) The permission under subsection (1) of this section shall not be extended to the reproduction—

(a) of a work of architecture in the form of a building or other constructions ;

(b) in the form of reprography of the whole or a substantial part of a book or of a musical work in the form of notations;

(c) of the whole or a substantial part of a data base;

(d) of a computer program, except as provided in subsection (7) ; and

(e) of any work, in case the reproduction would conflict with a normal exploitation of the work or would otherwise unreasonably prejudice the legitimate interests of the owner of the copyright.

(3) Notwithstanding the provisions of paragraph (a) of subsection (1) of section 9, the reproduction, in the form of a quotation, of a short part of a published work shall be permitted without authorization of the owner of copyright: Provided that the reproduction is compatible with fair practice and does not exceed the extent justified by the purpose of such reproduction. The quotation shall be accompanied by an indication of the source and the name of the author, if his name appears in the work from which the quotation is taken.

(4) Notwithstanding the provisions of paragraph (a) of subsection (1) of section 9, the following acts shall be

permitted without the authorization of the owner of the copyright:

(a) the reproduction of a short part of a published work for teaching purposes by way of illustration, in writing or sound or visual recordings, provided that the reproduction is compatible with fair practice and does not exceed the extent justified by the purpose of such reproduction;

(b) the reprographic reproduction for face to face teaching in any educational institution the activities of which do not serve direct or indirect commercial gain, of published articles, other short works or short extracts of works, to the extent justified by the purpose, provided that the act of reproduction is an isolated one occurring, if repeated, on separate and unrelated occasions:

Provided however the source of the work reproduced and the name of the author shall be indicated as far as practicable on all copies made under this subsection.

(5) Notwithstanding the provisions of paragraph (a) of subsection (1) of section 9, any library or archives, whose activities do not serve any direct or indirect commercial gain may, without the authorization of the owner of copyright, make a single copy of the work by reprographic reproduction—

(a) where the work reproduced is a published article, other short work or short extract of a work, and where the purpose of the reproduction is to satisfy the request of a physical person: Provided that—

(i) the library or archives is satisfied that the copy will be used solely for the purposes of study, scholarship or private research,

(ii) the act of reproduction is an isolated occurrence, occurring if repeated, on separate and unrelated occasions;

(b) where the copy is made in order to preserve and, if necessary replace a copy, or to replace a copy which has been lost, destroyed or rendered unusable in the permanent collection of another similar library or archives: Provided that it is not possible to obtain such a copy under reasonable conditions; and Provided further, that the act of reprographic reproduction is an isolated occurrence occurring if repeated, on separate and unrelated occasions.

(6) Notwithstanding the provisions of paragraphs (a), (h) and (j) of subsection (1) of section 9, and subject to the condition that the source and the name of the author is indicated as far as practicable, the following acts shall be permitted in respect of a work without the authorization of the owner of copyright—

(a) the reproduction in a newspaper or periodical, manner of broadcasting or other manner of communication to the public, of an article published in a newspaper or periodical on current economic, political or religious topics or a broadcast or communication relating to the same, and such permission shall not apply where the right to authorize reproduction, broadcasting or other communication to the public is expressly reserved on the copies, by the owner of copyright, or in connection with broadcasting or other communication to the public of the work;

(b) for the purpose of reporting current events, the reproduction and the broadcasting or other communication to the public of short excerpts of a work seen or heard in the course of such events, to the extent that it is justified by the purpose of such reproduction;

(c) the reproduction in a newspaper or periodical, broadcasting or other manner of communication to the public, of a political speech, a lecture, address, sermon or other work of a similar nature delivered in public, or a speech delivered during legal proceedings, to the extent that it is justified by reason of the fact of providing current information.

(7) (a) Notwithstanding anything contained in paragraphs (a) and (c) of subsection (1) of section 9, reproduction in a single copy or the adaptation of a computer program by the lawful owner of a copy of that computer programme, shall be permitted without the authorization of the owner of copyright provided that the copy or adaptation is necessary—

(i) for use of the computer program with a computer for the purpose and extent for which the computer program has been obtained;

(ii) for archival purposes and for replacement of the lawfully owned copy of the computer program in the event that the said copy of the computer program is lost, destroyed or rendered unusable.

(b) No copy or adaptation of a computer program shall be used for any purpose other than those specified in paragraph (a), and any such copy or adaptation shall be destroyed in the event that continued possession of the copy of the computer program ceases to be lawful.

(8) Notwithstanding the provisions of paragraph (f) of subsection (1) of section 9, the importation of a copy of a work by a physical person for his own personal purposes shall be permitted without the authorization of the owner of copyright.

(9) Notwithstanding anything contained in paragraph (g) of subsection (1) of section 9, the public display of originals or copies of works shall be permitted without the authorization of the owner of copyright: Provided that the display is made other than by means of a film, slide, television image or otherwise on screen or by means of any other device or process : Provided further, the work has been published or the original or the copy

displayed has been sold, given away or otherwise transferred to another person by the author or his successor in title.

(10) Notwithstanding anything contained in this Part, the following shall not be an infringement of copyright:

(a) the performance or display of a work for educational or teaching purposes by government or nonprofit educational institutions, in classrooms or similar places set aside for education : Provided that, in the case of an audiovisual work, the performance or the display of individual images, is given by means of a lawfully made copy, or the person responsible for the performance did not know or had no reason to believe that the copy was not lawfully made.

(b) the communication of a transmission embodying a performance or display of a work by the public reception of the transmission on a single receiving apparatus, of a kind commonly used in private homes, unless:

   (i) a direct charge is made to see or hear the transmission ; or

   (ii) the transmission thus received is further transmitted to the public.

7
Fair Use Guidelines

"The world goes ahead because each of us builds on the work of our predecessors. 'A dwarf standing on the shoulders of a giant can see farther than the giant himself.' Progress would be stifled if the author had a complete monopoly of everything in his book ....".

The doctrine of fair use need not be so mysterious or dependent on intuitive judgments. Fair use should be perceived not as a disorderly basket of exceptions to the rules of copyright, nor as a departure from the principles governing that body of law, but rather as a rational, integral part of copyright, whose observance is necessary to achieve the objectives of that law

— Honorable Judge Pierre N. Leval, of the United States Court of Appeals for the Second Circuit

7.0 Introduction

Fair use of fair dealing doctrine is considered as the *Safety Valve* of the copyright law. It is intended to allow people to use copyrighted materials without acquiring a license or permission from the creator for purposes such as personal use, criticism, comment, news reporting, teaching (including multiple copies for classroom use), scholarship, or research. One of the great copyright scholars Justice Pierre N. Leval said that *the copyright is not an inevitable, divine, or natural right that confers on authors the absolute ownership of their creations. It is designed rather to stimulate activity and progress in the arts for the intellectual enrichment of the public. This utilitarian goal is achieved by permitting authors to reap the rewards of their creative efforts. [C]opyright is intended to increase and not to impede the harvest of knowledge. . . . The rights conferred by copyright are designed to assure contributors to the store of knowledge a fair return for their labors.* Fair use is primarily meant for rewriters for their derivative works on the original copyrighted works. When the copyright act came in 1790 there was no conception of derivative works. Now the derivative works are independently copyrightable. Thinkers argue that as the horizons of copyrights have been expanded along with the inception of information and communication technologies so the protective umbrella of fair use must be expanded to embrace the change. Some legal scholars rightly said that fair use itself defies definition which should be taken as an opportunity rather a challenge. This opportunity can be used sensibly in the university system to advance its mission. Section 52 of the Indian Copyright Act has enumerated many such opportunities which can be used sensibly in favor of us to act as guideline. This guideline can be helpful not only for the universities but also for any Higher Educational Institutions (HEIs) of our country.

7.1. Common Fair Use Myths

The *Centre for Social Media of Temple University, US* in its Code of Best Practices in Fair Use for Media Literacy Education enumerated few myths regarding fair use which are equally applicable and relevant in Indian universities also.

1. *Myth* : Fair Use Is Too Unclear and Complicated

Truth : *The fair use provision of the Copyright Act is written broadly—not narrowly—because it is designed to apply to a wide range of creative works and the people* *who use them. Fair use is a part of the law that belongs to everyone—especially to working educators. Educators know best what they need to use of existing copyrighted culture to construct their own lessons and materials.*

2. *Myth* : If I'm not making Any Money off It, It's Fair Use.

Truth : *Non-commercial use is indeed one of the considerations for fair use, but it is hard to define. If people want to share their work only with a defined closed-circle group, they are in a favorable legal position. But beyond that, in the digital online environment, wholesale copying can be unfair even if no money changes hands.*

3. *Myth* : Educators Can Rely On "Rules of Thumb" For Fair Use Guidance

Truth : *Fair use is situational, and context is critical. Because it is a tool to balance the rights of users with the rights of owners, educators need to apply reason to reach a decision. The principles and limitations above are designed to guide your reasoning and to help you guide the reasoning of others.*

4. *Myth* : Fair Use Is Just For Critiques, Commentaries, or Parodies.

Truth : *Transformativeness, a key value in fair use law, can involve modifying material or putting material in a new context, or both. Fair use applies to a wide variety of purposes, not just critical ones. Using an appropriate excerpt from copyrighted material to illustrate a key idea in the course of teaching is likely to be a fair use, for example. Indeed, the Copyright Act itself makes it clear that educational uses will often be considered fair because they add important pedagogical value to referenced materials.*

5. *Myth* : Fair Use Is A Right.

Truth : *Copyright scholars say based on the language, it could be argued that the fair dealing provisions under the Indian Copyright Act are not a right but a defense or an exception.*

6. *Myth* : Employing Fair Use Is Too Much Trouble; I Don't Want To Fill Out Any Forms.

Truth **:** *Users who claim fair use simply use copyrighted works after making an assessment of the particular situation—there's nothing formal or official to "do" to claim fair use. You do not have to ask permission or alert the copyright holder when considering a use of materials that is protected by fair use.*

7. *Myth* : Fair Use Could Get Me Sued.

Truth **:** *That's very, very unlikely. Before even considering a lawsuit, a copyright owner typically will take the cheap and easy step of sending a "cease and desist" letter, sometimes leading the recipient to think that she is being sued rather than just threatened. An aggressive tone does not necessarily mean that the claims are legitimate or that a lawsuit will be filed.*

8. *Myth* : If I Try To License Material, I've Given Up My Chance To Use Fair Use.

Truth **:** *Everyone likes to avoid conflict and reduce uncertainty, and a maker may choose to seek permissions even in situations where they may not be required. Later, a maker still may decide to employ fair use. The fact that a license was requested–or even denied–doesn't undercut an otherwise valid fair use claim.*

7.2. Guideline for Classroom

Guideline for fair dealing in the classroom may take a shape of these following questions like-

(a) Will the work be used in closed academic setting?

(b) Is the purpose of using the work is truly academic or educational?

(c) Will the student's education benefit from this use?

(d) Was the copy of the work obtained legally?

(e) Are you distributing any printed copyrighted material beyond the conventional limit say for example 10% of the document?

(f) Are you electronically distributing any copyrighted file meant for private use only which may adversely affect the potential market of the document in question?

No other purposes other than academic or educational is permissible and eventually it may attract infringement which is a costly proposition for any academic institution. We should keep in mind that four factors of fair use analysis (*as discussed in the chapter 2*) but complying these four factors can keep us in the right side of the law. Try to use the materials covered under Creative Commons (CC) and Public Domain (PD) instead of copyrighted ones in classroom which will reduce the risk of unnecessary litigation.

Prof. Kenneth D. Crews, a great copyright scholar very beautifully presented the history of fair use guidelines in classroom situation in a seminal paper *the Law of Fair Use and the Illusion of Fair Use Guidelines* in 2001.

The earliest example of such a fair-use guideline was the so-called "Gentlemen's Agreement" of 1935 that identified instances of reproduction of short copyrighted works that would be allowed under the law at that time.... The best known of all fair-use guidelines emerged in 1976, not coincidentally in conjunction with the passage of the newly revised Copyright Act. For the first time, the law embodied fair use in statutory terms, and not merely as a judicial doctrine. To many copyright proprietors—particularly publishers—the newly codified fair use was a challenge or even a threat.

It's undeniable that our higher education system is suffering from lack of awareness of copyright and this is reflected in our classrooms also. In spite of close relationship between fair use, scholarship and teaching–learning but there is hardly any rules or guidelines to promote fair use. Fair use aware university community not only lessen the possibility of unnecessary litigation but also creates a healthy ambience for creativity and scholarship.

7.3. Guideline for Faculty Members

The Right to Education has been included in the Directive Principles of State Policy of Indian Constitution. India was first a signatory to the Berne Convention, which specifically recognizes an exception for "teaching purposes" in Article 10 (2). This article, now known as the teaching exception, was incorporated into the TRIPS (Trade Related Aspects of Intellectual Property Rights) Agreement through article 9(1) of TRIPS which provides that:

It shall be a matter for legislation in the countries of the Union, and for special agreements existing or to be concluded between them, to permit the utilization, to the extent justified by the purpose, of literary or artistic works by way of illustration in publications, broadcasts or sound or visual recordings for teaching, provided that such utilization is compatible with fair practice.

India is also TRIPS signatory and complies its obligations for teaching exceptions through its Section 52 of the Indian Copyright Act. Now let us analyze the functional aspects for guiding faculty members practicing fair dealing while discharging their services.

For many faculty members, duplicated material is the mainstay of the lesson plan. Without the ability to copy and distribute the ideas, writings, charts and diagrams created by experts in various fields, today's professor would quickly experience a credibility gap with students. Text books, once the central focus of the college classroom, must now be supplemented with materials desirable for specialized and contemporary content. Professors should utilize the benefits as offered in the section 52 (h) (i, ii & iii) of the Indian Copyright Act in favor of them as well as for students.

7.3.1. Uploading learning material/ scholarly material

While faculty members are uploading any learning material or articles in their personal blog/ web site/ institutional repository/ digital archive meant for facilitating in learning should take care of the following issues:

1. Learning materials in any format are available only to limited and bonafide users with strict authentication system.
2. If they are uploading anything downloaded from the university library resources as digital files or scanned copy from the analog document must consult both the university librarian and the copyright officer of the university.
3. Raise awareness among students /scholars regarding the use and distribution restriction of the learning materials downloaded from the site in question.

7.3.2. In the Classroom

Fair dealing is judged case by case basis and it is very contextual. Thus before you any copyrighted works for classroom instruction and unsure about fairness in dealing you may self-check the following points for own certainty:

1. Will the work be used in the classroom or closed academic setting only?
2. Is the work fact or fiction? (Fact has better possibility of being fair dealing)
3. Was the material used considering its qualitative and quantitative copying?
4. Will the present use adversely impact the potential market of the copyrighted works?

5. Did you transform the wo'k for repurposing?

Answer should be in the following in order to fall under the ambit of fair dealing:

1. Yes
2. Fact
3. Quantitative only within 10% of the works conventionally
4. No
5. Yes

To ensure fair dealing one may further refer to Chapter 2 -Concept of Fair Use (Section *2.5.1 Checklist for Fair use).*

7.4. Guideline for Scholars and Students

Academic ethics, integrity, sanctity of knowledge and purity of creation are most important elements needed among students, scholars or anyone belong to university academic community that help practicing fair dealing in the university and keep them in the right side of the law. Let me give an example which may clear the issue said. Suppose, you have arrived to a house which is full of valuables but owner of the house is not in the vicinity. Valuables may trigger some sort of temptation of lifting among a few. Do you think is it morally correct to lift some valuables from the house as the house owner is not there? If your answer is 'no' then you will be always in the right side of the law. Owner of the copyrighted works may be unseen and invisible to us but using their treasures or creative works beyond the limit set by the law is unfair like lifting of any valuables in the absence of the house owner. This is the basic principle to keep oneself within the fair dealing while you are using others copyrighted works. In Indian condition, it is said that primarily due to poor affordability of our students and scholars sometimes force them to go beyond the fair dealing. Not that it is incorrect in some cases, but plethora of examples can be cited in contrary to that when students and scholars habitually resorted to unfair dealing of the copyrighted works in spite of their adequate affordability. Once you start practicing fair dealing you will be habituated with that. If we make our students and scholars including ourselves aware regarding fair dealing we can avoid infringements and needless litigation. Following are few basic activities where normally copyrighted works may be used by the Students and scholars like:

1. Photocopy of library printed books and journals
2. Download of library ebooks and ejournals
3. Distribution of photocopies among friends and peers
4. Electronic distribution of digital copy of books and journal files among friends and peers
5. Electronic distribution of other copyrighted works like large data set, bibliographic data files, video clips and many other types of presentation, audio and video files.
6. Use of copyrighted works in preparing the assignments, presentation and other media files
7. Use of copyrighted works in writing research reports, articles, dissertations or theses

The following guideline is purely indicative in nature but not exhaustive.

A determination will be made as to whether the proposed use fall within the Fair Dealing of section 52 of the Indian Copyright Act, considering all of the relevant circumstances, including:

(a) the purpose of the proposed copying, including whether it is for research, private study, criticism, review, news reporting, parody, satire, answering examination paper or education;

(b) the character of the proposed copying, including whether it involves single or multiple copies, and whether the copy is destroyed after it is used for its specific intended purpose;

(c) the amount of the dealing from the individual user's perspective, including the proportion of the Work that is proposed to be copied and the importance of that excerpt in relation to the whole Work;

(d) alternatives to copying the Work, including whether there is a non-copyrighted equivalent available like licensed under Creative Commons (CC) or in the public domain;

(e) the nature of the Work, including whether it is published or unpublished; and

(f) the effect of the copying on the Work, including whether the copy will compete with the commercial market of the original Work.

If you are still unsure whether your use is fair or unfair you must refer it to Chapter 2 -Concept of Fair Use (Section *2.5.1 Checklist for Fair use).*

7.5. Guideline for Other Staff Members

Any member of the university community or any staff member like to use any copyrighted works from library or any licensed e-resources from the library or information resource centre need to follow the same path suggested for faculty members, students or research scholars.

7.6. Framework for Copyright Analysis

To deal with uncertainty and to determine the fair dealing, renowned copyright scholar *Kevin L. Smith, Director, Copyright and Scholarly Communication of Duke University and Ann T. Gilliland of University of North Carolina at Chapel Hill* suggested a framework for copyright consisting of the following five questions, in the order they are presented. They are simple questions, but they are not easy to answer. This framework can be of use by faculty members, students including research scholars and any staff members of the university.

The five questions that form this framework for copyright analysis are:

1. Is the work protected by copyright?
   a. Is the work I want to use protected by copyright, or is it in the public domain?
   b. If I wrote it, do I still own copyright, or did I sign over rights for my intended use to the publisher?
2. Is there a specific exception in copyright law that covers my use?
   a. Is my intended use covered by a specific exception to the exclusive rights in the copyright law, such as the one for libraries or for classroom performances and displays?
3. Is there a license that covers my use?
   a. Is there a Creative Commons license attached to the work? If so, can I comply with the terms of the license, or can I find another useful work that is CC-licensed?
   b. If affiliated with an educational institution, is there a license that governs how the copyrighted material I'm accessing through my library can be used? If so, can I comply with the license terms? If you are uncertain, your librarian should be able to help you.
4. Is my use covered by fair use?
   a. Four factors are:
      i. the purpose and character of the use, including whether such use is of a commercial nature or is for non-profit educational purposes;
      ii. the nature of the copyrighted work;

iii. the amount and substantiality of the portion used in relation to the copyrighted work as a whole; and

iv. the effect of the use upon the potential market for or value of the copyrighted work.

b. Questions for transformative fair use under factor one are:

i. Does the copyrighted material help me make my new point?

ii. Will it help my readers or viewers get my point?

iii. Have I used no more than is needed to make my point? (Is it "just right"?)

5. Do I need permission from the copyright owner for my use?

a. If so, first locate the copyright owner and fully explain your intended use in your permission request.

b. If no response or answer is no, reconsider your use of this work to see if you can make a fair use, or consider using another work.

One can evaluate his or her uses of copyrighted materials online. However, it is based on US copyright code. Following online tool is created by ALA (American Library Association). One can use the tool online here *librarycopyright.net/resources/fairuse/*

7.7. Reshaping a Fairer Future...

Confusions and fear of needless juridical exercises regarding the use of copyrighted works put universities sometimes unsettled and undermined across the country. Indian higher education system is maturing towards world class system and this calls for more consciousness and awareness about the rights of the creators or authors and the rights of the users too. Better and quality higher education means promotion of fair dealing of copyright works to stimulate creativity and innovation.

The most effective copyright management policy guidelines will emerge from cooperation and concerted efforts from all stakeholders, not confrontation. Policymakers should not always insist on exact answer to all copyright related disputes because sometimes determining the rights and prediction of future needs become very difficult to fathom. It is better sometime some copyright questions left answered. This might be resolved case by case after holistic examination of the issues involved guided by the general principles and spirits of copyright law.

No policy serve forever rather it's a dynamic force that changes dynamically with the time. With the change of technological milieu and new socio-economic and cultural demand in the society, policy should embrace those changes to serve the society better and adopt those changes. Any model policy that emerges from negotiations by all stakeholders should be scheduled for periodic reviews. Periodic reviews can also instill a new spirit of copyright law and the relationship of fair use to the academic mission and to encourage of creativity and innovation among the academic community. Model copyright management policy in the universities should aim at foster creativity and excellence. Any policy including copyright management policy should supplement the core mission of the university i.e., advancement of learning and promotion of scholarship.

Dispute, confusion, disagreement and even tension may arise out of the use of any copyrighted works by faculty members, students, scholars and staff or in the course of discharging their service to the university. Everything can be resolved by properly defining responsibilities and rights which will not only minimize the copyright conflict but also help evolving a balanced copyright management policy.

New content, new perspectives, new court verdicts, new amendments, new media, new technology for creation, storage and distribution, new interest and new uses of copyrighted works must be reflected while reinventing, redefining and reframing the university copyright management policy for the future so that its compliance should not be felt as a burden by the university community but an academic necessity to respect the legal aspects of creation and its fair dealing for further creation.

Annexures

Annexure I : Statement of Copyright Compliance

Faculty and Teaching Staff, Researchers and Students

The University of .... (*Name of the University*) .... has a responsibility to ensure that the rights of the creators of copyright materials are respected and that they are appropriately compensated for the use of their materials.

The university is responsible for ensuring reasonable effort has been exercised to ensure all material that is distributed to students, researchers of all types (*JRF/ SRF/ URF/ Project Staff/ RA/ any registered scholars for M.Phil or PhD or D.Lit or D.Sc or any one comes under the definition of researcher or scholar of the concerned university*) is compliant with current legislation and licensing agreements into which we have entered.

Teaching staff and faculty (*or anyone who comes under the definition of teaching staff of the concerned university*) have the responsibility to ensure the materials they are using in their courses are compliant with copyright law and with licensing agreements into which the university has entered.

The University requires all students, researchers, faculty and teaching staff who use and distribute materials for academic purposes need to complete the appended *Copyright Clearance Form* and to provide this Form to the Dean, Department Head, or Director, as the case may be, together with the course syllabus and the following acknowledgment. Any student, researcher or faculty member or teaching staff who has questions regarding the Copyright Clearance Forms should contact the Copyright Coordinator at 000-0000 or *copyright.coordinator@univ.ac.in*

"I acknowledge and understand my responsibility under the Use of Materials Protected by the Indian Copyright Act and have used reasonable efforts to complete the Copyright Clearance Forms in compliance with my responsibilities under that the Act. The Copyright Clearance Forms contain all the materials that are used and distributed both in hard copy and electronically".

Date : .... Signature : ....

Name : ....

Course : ....

Please complete this form and the *Copyright Clearance Forms* **every Semester** and forward them, together with the course syllabus, to your Dean, Department Head, or Director, as applicable.

Annexure II

Copyright Clearance Form

Name of the User:

Course:

Faculty along with the Department:

Semester:

Please be advised that this form must be completed and submitted to the Department Head / Dean of the Faculty.

Express Permission for your intended use

Title of publication (s)	Title of Excerpt (if applicable)	Publisher	ISBN/ISSN (if applicable)	Author(s)	Editor(s) (if applicable)	Distribution medium (electronic/ hardcopy)	*(If electronic)* Method of Distribution (e.g. Blackboard, personal website)	File name (*if uploaded in any electronic medium*)	Has a license already been obtained? (Yes or No)*

I have reasonably investigated and satisfied myself that the use of the copyrighted material (s) is/are pursuant of Section 52 of the Indian Copyright Act and also true to my belief and knowledge I take the responsibility that any use contrary to that will liable for suitable action by the appropriate authority.

Signature of the Applicant

Annexure III : Sample Letter Requesting Permission to Reproduce Copyrighted Material

[Author]
[Publisher]
[Address]

Dear ________________,

I am writing to ask your permission to (check all that apply)

— reprint
— photocopy
— digitize
— incorporate into
    — course materials
    — online course materials
    — a dissertation/thesis
    — a website publication

the following material:

Author:

Title:

Vol: Issue:

Page (s): Figure/Image (s:) Table (s):

Minutes:

The material will be distributed/published as follows:

- Purpose: [Not-for-profit, educational]
- Format:
- Number of Copies:
- Distribution/Access:

If you do not control copyright in the requested materials, I would appreciate any information you can provide about others to whom I should write, including most recent address if available.

Sincerely,

(Signature of Applicant)

Permission Granted

I have the authority to grant the permission requested herein and I hereby grant .... permission to use the above referenced material in the manner described.

I request that the credit line read:

____

____

Copyright Holder's Signature

____

Author's Name

____

____

____

Address

____

Date

References

Band, J., & Gerafi, J. (n.d.). Fair Use/Fair Dealing Handbook. SSRN Electronic Journal SSRN Journal. doi:10.2139/ssrn.2333863

Bansal, A. (2012, September 22). To Copy or Not to Copy. Open Magazine. Retrieved October 1, 2012, from http://www.openthemagazine.com/article/india/to-copy-or-not-to-copy

Boyer, E. (1990) *Scholarship Reconsidered: Priorities of the professoriate.* New Jersey: The Carnegie Foundation for the Advancement of Teaching.

Braxton, J. M., Luckey, W., & Helland, P. (2002) Institutionalizing a broader view of scholarship through Boyer's four domains, *ASHE-ERIC Higher Education Report,* Vol. 29, No. 2. San Francisco: Jossey-Bass/John Wiley Periodicals.((

Brown, Richard. "From the University Presses-The Code of Best Practices in Fair Use for Academic and Research Libraries." Against the Grain 24.4 (2016): n. pag. Web.

Burk, D. L., & Cohen, J. E. (2001). Fair Use Infrastructure for Copyright Management Systems. *SSRN Electronic Journal SSRN Journal,* 41-83. doi:10.2139/ssrn.239731

Cochran, W. G. (2006). Sampling techniques. New York: J. Wiley.

Commission on Intellectual Property Rights (2002) Intellectual Property and Development. *Integrating Intellectual Property Rights and Development Policy* [online],13-15. Available from: http://www.iprcommission.org/papers/pdfs/final_report/CIPRfullfinal.pdf [Accessed 4th may 2011]

Copyright and Fair Use in the Classroom, on the Internet, and the World Wide Web - UMUC. (n.d.). Retrieved February 15, 2013, from http://glotta.ntua.gr/nlp/IS-Social/CopyRight/copy.html

Cornish, G. P. (n.d.). Copyright: Interpreting the law for libraries, archives and information services.

Crews, K. D. (1997). Fair Use and Higher Education: Are Guidelines the Answer? Academe, 83(6), 38. doi:10.2307/40251192

Crews, K. D. (2001). The Law of Fair Use and the Illusion of Fair-Use Guidelines. Ohio State Law Journal, 62, 602-700. doi:10.2139/ssrn.1588292

Crews, K. D. (2012). Copyright Law for Librarians and Educators Creative Strategies and Practical Solutions, Third Edition. Chicago: ALA Editions.

Crews, K. D., (1993). *Copyright, Fair Use, and the Challenge for Universities: Promoting the Progress of Higher Education.*. 1st ed. Chicago: University of Chicago Press.

Darch, C., Halbert, D. J., & Story, A. (2006). Copy / South dossier: Issues in the economics, politics, and ideology of copyright in the global South. Canterbury, U.K.: Copy/South Research Group.

Deazley, R., Kretschmer, M., & Bently, L. (2010). Privilege and property: Essays on the history of copyright. Cambridge, U.K.: OpenBook.

Fisher, W. (March 19, 2015). CopyrightX: Lecture 9.3, Fair Use: Other Approaches [Motion Picture On You Tube Video]. US: You Tube.

Garg, A. (2016, September 17). HC: Copyright is not a divine right, photocopying no crime. The Times of India (Kolkata). Retrieved September 17, 2016, from http://epaperbeta.timesofindia.com/Article.aspx?eid=31812&articlexml=HC-Copyright-is-not-a-divine-right-photocopying-17092016010025

Glenny, L. A., and Dalglish, T. K. (1973). Higher Education and the Law . *In* : J. A. Perkins, (ed) *University as an Organization.* New York, McGraw Hill Book Company. P.173-202

Governemnt of India (2004). *The Copyright Act, 1957.* New Delhi: Universal book Publishing. 34-35

Harper, G, (1993). *Copyright & the University Community.* 1st ed. Texas: The Office of General Counsel.

Hobbs, R. (2008). Code of Best Practices in Fair Use for Media Literacy Education. Washington: Centre for Social Media of Temple University, US.

Indian Copyright Act, 1957. (n.d.). Retrieved April 3, 2013, from http://copyright.gov.in/Documents/CopyrightRules1957.pdf

Leval, P. N. (1990). Toward a Fair Use Standard. Harvard Law Review, 103(5), 1105. doi:10.2307/1341457

Liang, L. (2010). Exceptions and Limitations in Indian Copyright Law for Education: An Assessment. The Law and Development Review, 3(2). doi:10.2202/1943-3867.1058

Matthan R., & Narendran N. (2011). Fair Dealing of Computer Programs in India. The Indian Journal of Law and Technology, 7, 91-102. Retrieved March 11, 2016.

Merrill, S. A., & Mazza, A. (2011). Managing university intellectual property in the public interest.

Washington, D.C.: National Research Council, National Academy Press.

Norman, S. (2004). Practical copyright for information

professionals: The CILIP handbook. London: Facet Publishing.

Pedley, P. (2007). Digital copyright. London: Facet Publishing.

Pedley, P. (2008). Copyright compliance: Practical steps to stay within the law. London: Facet.

Population Reference Bureau. (2011). World Population Data Sheet 2011. Available: www.prb.org/pdf11/2011population-data-sheet_eng.pdf. Last accessed 21th July 2011.

Rajagopal, K. (2008, September 22). Hari Puttar: HC dismisses Warner Bros' plea. The Indian Express. Retrieved September 27, 2008, from http://archive.indianexpress.com/news/hari-puttar-hc-dismisses-warner-bros—plea/364727/

Research Guides: Copyright at the University Library: Fair Dealing Guidelines. (n.d.). Retrieved September 05, 2015, from http://libguides.usask.ca/copyright/fairdealing

Roof, J. (1992). The Ideology of Fair Use: Xeroxing and Reproductive Rights.Hypatia, 7(2), 63-73. doi:10.1111/j.1527-2001.1992.tb00885.x

Shulman, L.S. & Hutchings P. (1998) *About the scholarship of teaching and learning: The Pew scholars national fellowship program.* Menlo Park, CA: The Carnegie Foundation for the Advancement of Teaching.

Suthersanen, U. (2003). Copyright and Educational Policies: A Stakeholder Analysis. Oxford Journal of Legal Studies, 23(4), 585-609. doi:10.1093/ojls/23.4.585

The George Washington University. (n.d.). Retrieved July 07, 2014, from https://www.gwu.edu/copyright

The Law of Fair Use and the Illusion of Fair-Use Guidelines. (n.d.). Retrieved January 1, 2016, from http://moritzlaw.osu.edu/students/groups/oslj/files/2012/03/62.2.crews_.pdf

The Task Force on Higher Education and Society, The International Bank for Reconstruction and Development. (2000). *Higher Education in Developing Countries: peril and promise.* Available: www.accesstosuccess-africa.eu/web/images/literature/peril_and_promise.pdf. Last accessed 17th June 2011.

Townsend, E., (2003). Legal and Policy Responses to the Disappearing "Teacher Exception," or Copyright in the 21st Century University. . *Intellectual Property Review,* [Online]. 4(2), 209-256. Available at: http://mipr.umn.edu/archive/v4n2/townsend.pdf [Accessed 17 March 2011].

Yoo, E. (2000). How can the fair use doctrine be applied for the appropriate level of copyright protection in the global marketplace.

Index